THE
FIRST DAY
AT
GETTYSBURG

A Walking Tour

By James E. Thomas

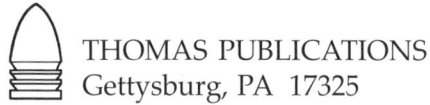
THOMAS PUBLICATIONS
Gettysburg, PA 17325

Cover illustration, *The Iron Brigade*, was painted by Don Troiani, www.historicalartprints.com.

Contents

Introduction

I heartily encourage you to take the time to walk on the battlefield! Obviously it is good physical exercise. And if you have to exercise, you might as well do it on a Civil War battlefield. In addition, walking gives you a totally new perspective on what happened here. It's the soldiers' perspective, and an unhurried perspective that allows your senses to take in much more than when you race around attempting to see the entire battlefield on a two-hour auto tour.

The regimental markers and the landscape also reveal many secrets to those taking the time to look. The monuments on the field, even when taken out of their military context, are beautiful works of art and are themselves worthy of the time it takes to view them. Each memorial has some form of stone carving and sculpture; still others feature bronze details, symbols, and in a few cases intricate bas reliefs. In many cases, the most interesting features of these stone memorials can't be seen from the park roads. The landscape is also much more impressive when experienced on foot. You'll realize that the battlefield is not as "flat" as it seems when viewed from an automobile or as illustrated in the maps found throughout history books. The rolling fields are dotted with stone walls, shady woods, streams, hay fields, wildlife and wildflowers. So I say again, get out and walk on the battlefield!

This tour book covers the entire First Day's battlefield. Actually containing three tours (A, B, and C), the battle area has been broken into manageable 2 to 3 mile routes. Proper foot wear is recommended. The tour routes do follow paved park roads, but excursions are provided that take you into the woods and fields. Caution also must be exercised when the tour route follows Chambersburg Pike, Fairfield Road, and the Old Harrisburg Road — these are high traffic areas.

This book is intended as a walking tour but is very adaptable to driving. Should you choose to drive, parking is available at or near most stops; the only exceptions are the stops located on Chambersburg Pike (Route 30). At the very end of the third tour, those driving will have to drive around the college campus when the walking tour goes through.

The accompanying text is not intended as a detailed study of the fighting on July 1, but rather as an overview to enable visitors to understand and appreciate this overlooked, yet very significant portion of the Gettysburg battlefield. A suggested reading list is provided at the back of the book for those who are interested in pursuing an indepth study of the first day's fight.

It is accepted that the significance of the first day's fighting has long been downplayed because the Northern troops "lost" the fight on July 1. The ground north and west of Gettysburg is also thought of as bland and featureless, at least compared with Little Round Top, Devil's Den, Cemetery Hill, and Culp's Hill. However, I disagree with these notions. Even a superficial study of the combat on July 1 shows how well most Federal units fought and how severe the fighting was in some locations. The first day's battlefield also has its share of significant topographical features: Oak Hill, Barlow's Knoll, the railroad bed with its many deep cuts, Gettysburg College's Pennsylvania Hall, the Old Dorm atop Seminary Ridge, Reynolds' (Herbst) Woods, Rock Creek and Willoughby Run. After taking these tours, hopefully you too will gain a new appreciation for the importance and ferocity of the first day's fighting at Gettysburg.

Thanks must be given to those people who contributed and assisted with this book: Garry Adelman, Tim Smith, Mike Vallone, Andy DeCusati, Truman Eyler, Mike Dreese, Tom Henrique, Wayne Motts and Dave Slemmer.

Life is not all about the Civil War and Gettysburg. So I heartily acknowledge the wonderful people who do make my life complete — Ellen, my wife; Jim, Sarah, Zach, and Kate, my children; and Dean, my big brother — I'm blessed that these special people are a part of my family.

The Battle Opens, July 1

Lieutenant General Ambrose P. Hill's Corps of Confederates began the day in and around Cashtown, nine miles west of Gettysburg. Major General Henry Heth led his division on what was expected to be an uneventful and pleasant march to Gettysburg for provisions. It was 5:00 a.m. on July 1, 1863.

As the Rebels approached the bridge over Marsh Creek (three miles from Gettysburg), one of the first shots of this battle was fired. Expecting a Confederate advance on July 1, Brigadier General John Buford made plans to hold Gettysburg with his Union cavalry until Major General John F. Reynolds' infantry could arrive and take over the fight. These plans included a cavalry picket line that guarded the approaches from the west and north. Lieutenant Marcellus Jones of the 8th Illinois Cavalry was the officer in charge of the advanced pickets on the Chambersburg Pike overlooking Marsh Creek. Upon seeing the approaching Southern column, Lt. Jones borrowed a Sharps carbine and fired at the approaching Confederates.

Brigadier General James J. Archer deployed portions of his brigade as skirmishers who swept toward the Yankees. By fighting and then falling back from ridge to ridge, the dismounted troopers helped stall the Confederate advance. Eventually the Northern pickets fell back upon their main line formed on the western portions of McPherson's Ridge and supported by Lieutenant John Calef's Battery A, 2nd U.S. Artil-

Battles and Leaders

lery. On finding the main battle line of the Yankees, the Confederates formed their own battle lines atop Herr's Ridge. Archer's Brigade formed south of the Chambersburg Pike (modern Rt. 30), while Brigadier General Joseph Davis formed his brigade to the north of the pike. Soon the Southern infantry was splashing across Willoughby Run.

Archer & Davis Attack McPherson's Ridge

So far the Confederates had spent about two hours trying to push aside the Union cavalry. The Southerners continued their advance at a steady pace. The Northern troopers were outnumbered, but able to compensate for this with their carbines. These breech-loading weapons used by the cavalry allowed a faster rate of fire than the infantry's muskets. Carbines were also easy to load from a prone or concealed position.

By 9:30 a.m., the Federal cavalry was losing control of the fight. South of the pike, Archer was close to taking Herbst Woods and gaining control of McPherson's Ridge. North of the pike, Davis advanced dispursing the cavalrymen facing him. But by that time the cavalry had already done what they needed to do — stall the Confederates until the Union infantry could reach the battlefield.

Finally the Union infantry began to arrive. Brigadier General Lysander Cutler's Brigade led the way. From Emmitsburg Road they crossed the fields to Seminary Ridge. They turned west once they reached the Seminary buildings. The infantrymen paused here giving Captain James Hall's 2nd Maine Battery a clear path as it raced to the front. Hall's guns replaced Calef's Battery, which had retired. Forming a line of battle, Cutler's infantrymen headed for McPherson's Ridge to support Hall's Battery. In the process, the brigade was split in two; three of the regiments eventually ended up north of an unfinished railroad bed while two regiments remained on the south side of the pike.

Next came Brigadier General Solomon Meredith's "Iron Brigade," which turned off Seminary Ridge at the Fairfield Road and then double-quicked through the low ground between Seminary and McPherson Ridges. This route was out of sight and provided cover from the artillery fire. General Reynolds himself urged on the leading regiment (the 2nd Wisconsin), getting them immediately into action against Archer's Confederates charging through Herbst Woods.

At this time, while directing the regiments of the Iron Brigade into action, Reynolds was struck in the head by a bullet and killed.

Archer's men were moving through Herbst Woods when suddenly the Iron Brigade struck them in front and flank. The Confederates recoiled back to Willoughby Run. Some tried to reform their ranks and resist but to no avail. Meredith's infantrymen overlapped the Rebel line and chased them back across Willoughby Run and up the slopes of Herr Ridge.

Heavy casualties were suffered by both sides, but the Confederates also lost about 300 men captured along with General Archer himself.

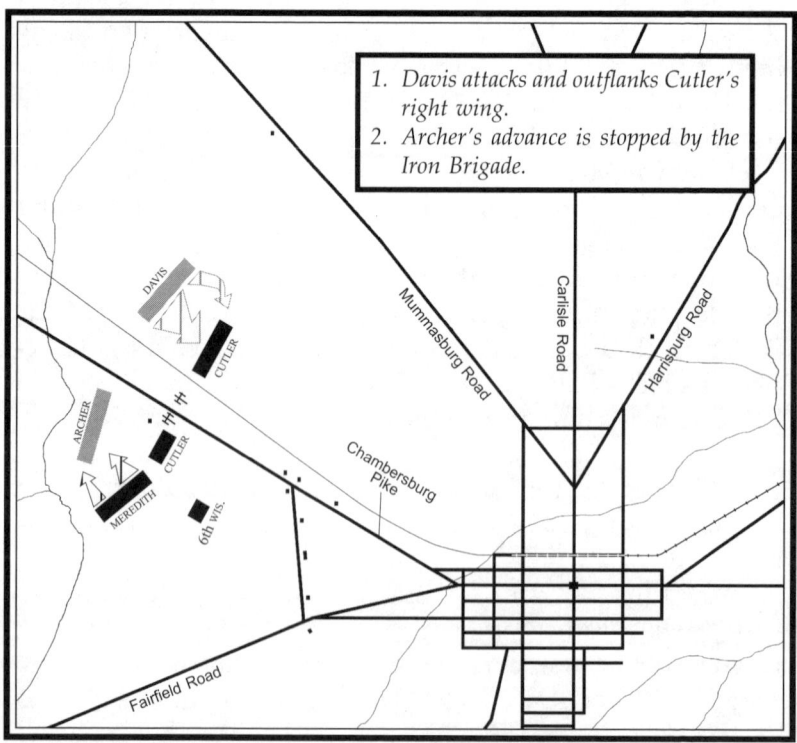

1. *Davis attacks and outflanks Cutler's right wing.*
2. *Archer's advance is stopped by the Iron Brigade.*

Battles and Leaders

North of the Pike, Davis' Confederates initially fared much better. His Mississippians and North Carolinians easily flanked two of the three Federal regiments, inflicting severe casualties and forcing their retreat. The third Federal regiment, the 147th New York, never received its orders to withdraw and remained in position supporting the right of Hall's Battery. Davis' whole brigade now turned on these Yankees and soon the remnants of the 147th New York and Hall's artillerymen were also making their escape as best they could.

Davis' Confederates were sweeping the field and in hot pursuit of the survivors of Cutler's Brigade north of the railroad bed. In doing so the Rebels were getting in the rear of the Union forces south of the Pike. Seeing this danger, General Doubleday ordered the 6th Wisconsin Infantry to attack. A volley from the 6th surprised the Rebels and caused Davis' three regiments to use the unfinished railroad bed for cover. However, the center of the Rebel line was in a portion of the railroad bed that passed through McPherson's Ridge. The resulting "railroad cut" was so deep that it was difficult to shoot out of. Instead of being a good defensive position, the railroad cut became a trap.

Cutler's two regiments posted south of the Pike (14th Brooklyn and 95th New York) also noticed the danger to their

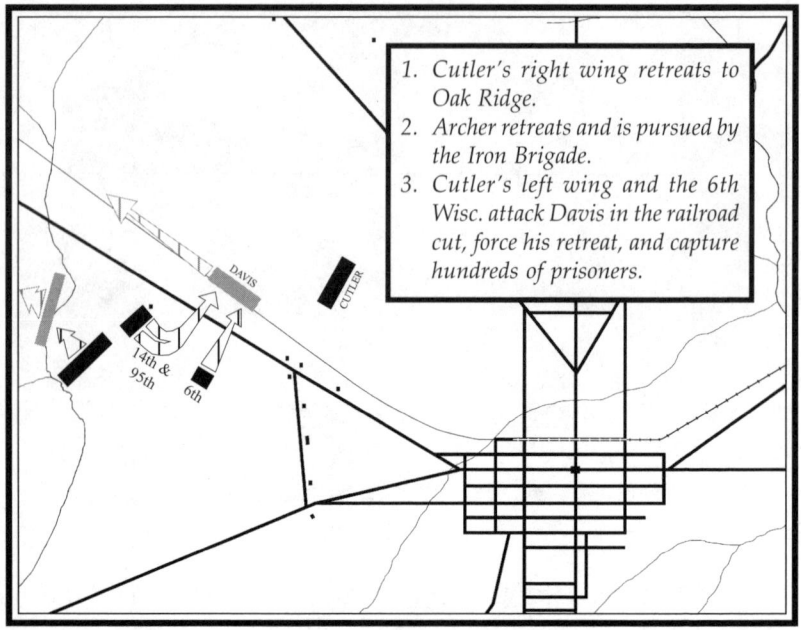

1. Cutler's right wing retreats to Oak Ridge.
2. Archer retreats and is pursued by the Iron Brigade.
3. Cutler's left wing and the 6th Wisc. attack Davis in the railroad cut, force his retreat, and capture hundreds of prisoners.

position. Without orders they too joined the attack on the Confederates in the railroad bed. After a desperate and bloody charge, the three Union regiments reached the edge of the "cut" and had the Confederates below at their mercy. About 300 Southerners were captured, mostly from the 2nd Mississippi. The unorganized remnants of Davis' Brigade made their way back toward Herr's Ridge any way they could.

After severe fighting, the attacks made by both Confederate brigades had been repulsed. It was around noon, and an uneasy quiet settled over the battlefield.

Rodes Attacks Oak Ridge

By two o'clock, Major General Robert Rodes' Division of Confederates had arrived on the field from the north and occupied Oak Hill. Leading elements of the Union 11th Corps and another 1st Corps brigade commanded by Brigadier General Henry Baxter arrived at approximately the same time with orders to extend the 1st Corps battle line. The Federals now were in position along Oak Ridge all the way to the

Mummasburg Road. The Rebel occupation of Oak Hill ruined plans of anchoring the Union line there and instead would force them to extend their lines across the low plain north of Gettysburg. But there they would find themselves in the undesirable position of being under the Confederate guns on Oak Hill.

Rodes had five brigades in his division. He placed Brigadier General George Doles' Brigade on his left, out in the plain where they faced cavalry skirmishers and leading elements of the Union 11th Corps. From here Doles' Brigade operated somewhat independently from the division. Next was Colonel Edward O'Neal's Brigade just west of the crest of the ridge. Brigadier General Alfred Iverson's and Brigadier General Junius Daniel's Brigades were next in line to the west. Brigadier General Stephen Ramseur's Brigade was kept in reserve at the rear of the division.

Interpreting the arrival of Baxter's Brigade and the 11th Corps as preparations for an attack, Rodes decided to "beat them to the punch" and launch his own attack. The plan was to have three brigades advance on Oak Ridge simultaneously. However, poor communications, the nature of the terrain, and the simple fact that some units had greater distances to march had the effect of fragmenting one large attack into separate smaller fights. This gave the Yankees time and opportunity to shift positions and bring sufficient force to bear on each of the individual Southern attacks, easily defeating the first waves of Rodes' Confederates.

O'Neal's Brigade advanced on the Federal regiments posted at the Mummasburg Road. In short order O'Neal's attack was repulsed. In addition to the 1st Corps regiments in their front, the Alabamians received heavy fire from the east. Captain Hubert Dilger's Battery I, 1st Ohio Artillery and the 45th New York Infantry, the lead elements of the Union 11th Corps, were key ingredients in the quick failure of the attack.

Originally intended to support O'Neal's right, Iverson's Brigade found itself advancing alone due to the speed with which O'Neal was defeated. Iverson believed the assault would strike the flank of the Union line. Instead, Federal regiments of Baxter's Brigade were waiting, many behind a stone wall, for Iverson's unsuspecting soldiers. As the Confederates ap-

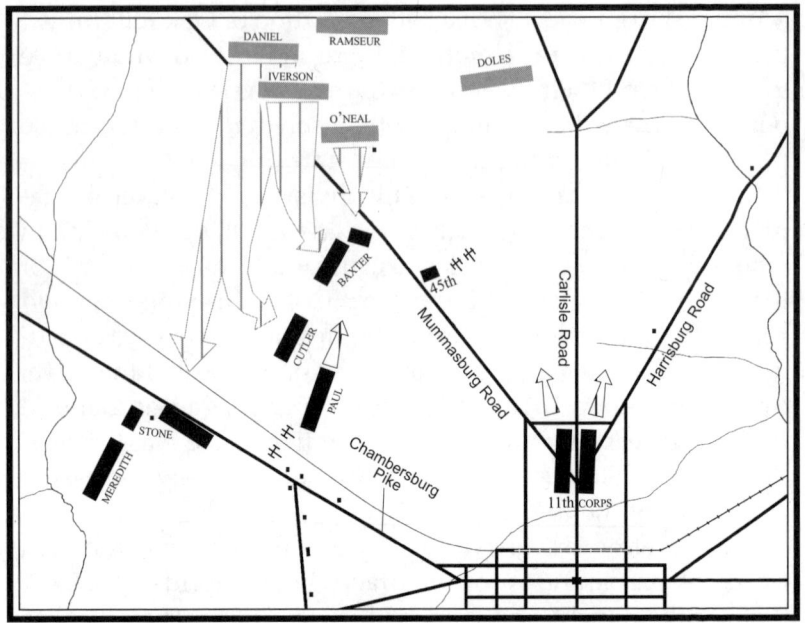

1. Rodes' Division and portions of the Union 11th Corps arrive.
2. Rodes attacks Union positions on Oak Ridge and along the Chambersburg Pike.
3. Paul's Brigade moves from the Seminary (where it had been building breastworks) to Baxter's aid near the Mummasburg Road.

proached, the Federals rose up and fired a devastating volley. The Confederate regiments were smashed.

The devastation and resulting disorganization was so complete that groups of Yankees were able to rush out amid the Rebels and capture flags and prisoners. The few survivors had to hug the ground; going to the front or rear meant sure death. But these survivors did manage to return fire and continue to occupy the attentions of the Union regiments on Oak Ridge while Daniel's and Ramseur's attacks unfolded.

Daniel's Brigade was supposed to support Iverson's right, extend the assault, and link up with Heth's forces to the west. But as Daniel advanced to support the attack, the situation on the field had changed. To the east Iverson's Brigade was being destroyed by the Federal troops of Baxter's Brigade. To the south Colonel Roy Stone's Brigade of Pennsylvanians, which had been added to the Union line on McPherson's Ridge, realigned along the Chambersburg Pike facing north to meet the new Confederate threats from Oak Hill.

By the time his brigade got into position to attack Oak Ridge, Daniel was taking fire from Stone's Brigade and Union batteries to the south. To protect his flank, Daniel split his brigade and attacked in two directions. Two of his regiments assaulted Oak Ridge, and three regiments headed for the Pennsylvanians along the Chambersburg Pike. Daniel's left regiments engaged Cutler's men in the woods on Oak Ridge to stop their firing into Iverson's already decimated brigade. Meanwhile, Daniel's remaining three regiments made two advances into and around the railroad cuts without success; Stone's Pennsylvanians counter-attacked and stopped the Southerners both times. Daniel prepared his tired soldiers for one more push.

By now it was evident to Rodes that he had to send in Ramseur's Brigade to help O'Neal and Iverson. Ramseur's four regiments were split into a left and a right wing. The left wing attacked on the eastern slope of Oak Ridge hoping to get around the end of the Union line. The right wing's attack headed for the stone wall south of the Mummasburg Road. O'Neal, after two fruitless assaults, rallied his men and pushed forward filling the space between Ramseur's two wings.

It was at this time that, finally, the Army of Northern Virginia's piecemeal attacks came together. Bringing their greater numbers to bear on the Union 1st and 11th Corps, they were beginning to make gains on the field, squeezing the Union Army back toward town.

The 11th Corps

Upon the death of General Reynolds, Major General Oliver O. Howard, who was commander of the 11th Corps, assumed command of the Union forces on the battlefield. Major General Carl Schurz was likewise elevated to command of the 11th Corps, leaving Brigadier General Francis C. Barlow in command of the 1st Division.

The 11th Corps was one of the weakest Corps in the Army of the Potomac. They were still recovering from the Battle of

Chancellorsville where they had suffered a crushing defeat that affected their strength and morale. Consisting of three divisions, each division had only two brigades. Compounding this weakness, on July 1, one division was held in reserve. The brigades that did fight were fed into the battle piecemeal or otherwise used ineffectively.

By early afternoon a brigade of the 11th Corps was already on the field, and soon the 1st and 3rd Divisions extended the Union battle line until it covered Gettysburg from the north all the way around to the Harrisburg Road; Brigadier General Adolph von Steinwehr's 2nd Division was held in reserve on Cemetery Hill.

Colonel George von Amsberg's Brigade was on the left of the 11th Corps line covering the fields between the Mummasburg and Carlisle Roads. Here they supported, but were not in direct contact with, the right of the Union 1st Corps. It was from this position that Dilger's Battery and the 45th New York poured a devastating fire into O'Neal's flank, greatly contributing to their quick defeat on the slopes of Oak Ridge.

Next in line to the right was Colonel Wladimir Krzyzanowski's Brigade. These regiments were positioned near the Carlisle Road. Krzyzanowski's men faced north, opposed by Doles' Brigade from Rodes' Division.

Brigadier General Adelbert Ames' and Colonel Leopold von Gilsa's brigades momentarily held a position in the vicinity of the Alms House. Brigadier General Francis Barlow (their division commander) quickly noticed higher ground to the northeast. Feeling it would be a good platform for his artillery, and fearing the knoll could be used effectively against him by Rebel artillery, Barlow advanced his division onto Blocher's Knoll. Major General Daniel Sickles would make a similar move, for similar reasons, and suffer a similar fate in the Peach Orchard the next day!

After the move and once fighting began, portions of Ames' Brigade were placed in line, also facing north. They extended the Union line from Krzyzanowski's Brigade to the high ground of Blocher's Hill where artillery was posted to cover the Harrisburg Road. Ames' men would suffer terribly from counter-battery fire the Confederates were directing at these Union cannons.

Colonel von Gilsa commanded the final brigade in the 11th Corps line. The brigade was facing northeast with the right of their line (and the 11th Corps) ending at the Harrisburg Road. Rather than keeping his men in their more effective regimental formations, von Gilsa placed most of his force along Rock Creek in a heavy skirmish line.

This is how the 11th Corps was positioned in the fields north of Gettysburg on the afternoon of July 1. They seemed to be preoccupied with Doles' Brigade advancing down the Carlisle Road and the possibility of attacking it. There were reports of Confederates on the Harrisburg Road, but none of the 11th Corps officers realized what the Confederates had in store for them. It would soon seem like Chancellorsville all over again!

Gordon & Doles attack

Confederate Major General Jubal Early had the good fortune to arrive on the field in the right place at the right time. Early's three brigades went into line of battle facing down the Harrisburg Road and threatening the right flank of the 11th Corps. Brigadier General John Gordon's Brigade of Georgians was positioned above the road, Brigadier General Harry Hayes' Louisianans were astride the road, and Colonel Isaac Avery's North Carolinians were below the road — some 4000 veteran soldiers.

Early used his artillery to soften Barlow's lines, then at about 3 o'clock Gordon's Brigade launched their attack on von Gilsa. When Doles saw Gordon advancing, he moved to join the fight. With this the Union regiments quickly found themselves in serious trouble with the Confederate fire hitting them from two directions. Ames' Brigade was fed in to strengthen weak spots in von Gilsa's line, but the Confederates continued to overlap the left and right of the Union defensive line. With men falling along the line, the 54th and 68th New York fell back leaving the 153rd Pennsylvania to face the Georgians. Casualties steadily mounted and the Federal line started to waiver. The Confederate advance was steady and, in Gordon's own words, "the brigade rushed upon the enemy with a reso-

lution and spirit...rarely excelled." At one critical moment the 75th Ohio and the 17th Connecticut regiments were ordered to charge over the crest of the knoll to check the Confederate assault. The two units were mauled and quickly forced to retreat as the entire division fell back toward the Alms House.

Krzyzanowski's Brigade tried to assist Barlow's overwhelmed division by advancing across the Carlisle Road and attacking the regiments on the right of Doles' Brigade. This Union attack was momentarily successful, forcing the 21st Georgia to retreat and providing an opportunity to flank the remainder of the Confederate brigade. However, this small "victory" came too late to stem the tide of Early's Division. With Barlow's two brigades in full retreat toward the Alms House, Doles' other regiments were able to disengage, change front, and deal with Krzyzanowski head on. The opposing brigades closed until about 75 yards separated them. They stood blasting away at each other with neither gaining an advantage. At this point, while most of his command continued their pursuit of Barlow's shattered division, two of Gordon's regiments faced to the right and fired into Krzyzanowski's line. This fire coming from the flank had a murderous effect on the Yankees. From right to left, each regiment in turn reeled from the Rebel bullets ripping down their lines. In about 15 min-

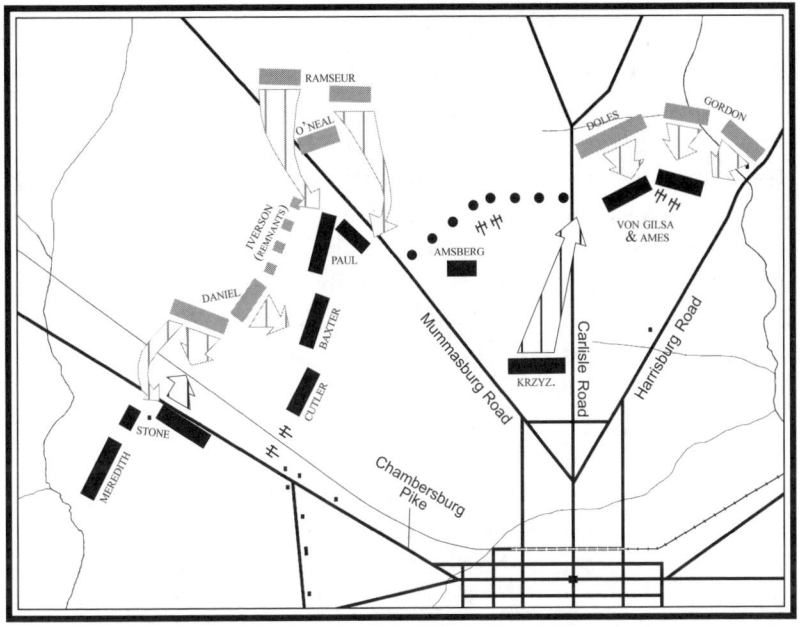

1. *Rodes continues his attacks on the Union 1st Corps.*
2. *Doles and Gordon attack Union positions on Blocher's Hill.*
3. *Krzyzanowski's Brigade moves to support Barlow's Division.*

utes the damage was done — the 26th Wisconsin, the 119th New York, and the 75th Pennsylvania each lost more than 100 men; the 82nd Ohio lost over half their regiment, or more than 150 men.

In still another attempt to check the Southern advances on the east side of Carlisle Road, the 157th New York was sent to support Krzyzanowski. Coming up to the road, the 157th New York struck the 44th Georgia square on their right flank. Fortunately for the 44th and 4th Georgia, Krzyzanowski was in full retreat, which allowed them to change front again and face this new threat. With impeccable timing the 12th and 21st Georgia appeared on the left flank of the 157th and opened fire. With the help of a battery on Oak Hill, the Confederates were now firing into this shrinking Federal regiment from all four directions. Within minutes the 157th was also retreating toward Gettysburg, leaving nearly 300 men behind.

Avery & Hays Finish the 11th Corps

Colonel Charles Coster's Brigade was released from its reserve position on Cemetery Hill to support Barlow's Division, which had been totally overwhelmed by Early's assault down the Harrisburg Road. Union artillery and remnants from Krzyzanowski and Ames made a stand on Carlisle Road. Coster formed his three regiments to the east of this demoralized band along a fence in Kuhn's Brickyard at the northeast edge of town. This location was problematic. Because of the terrain, there was a limited field of fire, and one end of the battle line could not see what was happening to the other.

Coster's regiments fought well, but not for long. Again it was too little too late. Early's troops had plenty of momentum and overlapped Coster's battleline on both ends. The weak ad hoc battleline at Carlisle Road was easily overrun, and two cannons were captured. At the brickyard, the 27th Pennsylvania quickly fell away under this same Confederate thrust. Unfortunately Coster's other regiments were not notified of the situation in that direction. In their front, the two New York regiments exchanged fire with Avery's North Carolinians; however, the 57th North Carolina's line extended far past that of the embattled Yankees. Rebels swept down on the front, the flank and wrapped around to the rear of the 134th New York. In short order, the regiment was crushed losing nearly 200 killed and wounded. By the time the 154th New York found out what had happened on the left and the right, they were all but surrounded. The situation quickly became one of "every man for himself." The 154th New York paid a terrible price for its brief stand, losing over 90 percent of its strength — almost all of this loss being captured men.

The remnants of the 11th Corps staggered back to Cemetery Hill with the Confederates on their heels.

Heth Finishes the 1st Corps

As Early's Confederates swept the Union 11th Corps from the plain north of Gettysburg, the right of the Union 1st Corps on Oak Ridge was also crumbling under the relentless attacks by several of Rodes' brigades. At this critical moment, Heth renewed his assault on McPherson's Ridge from the west. It

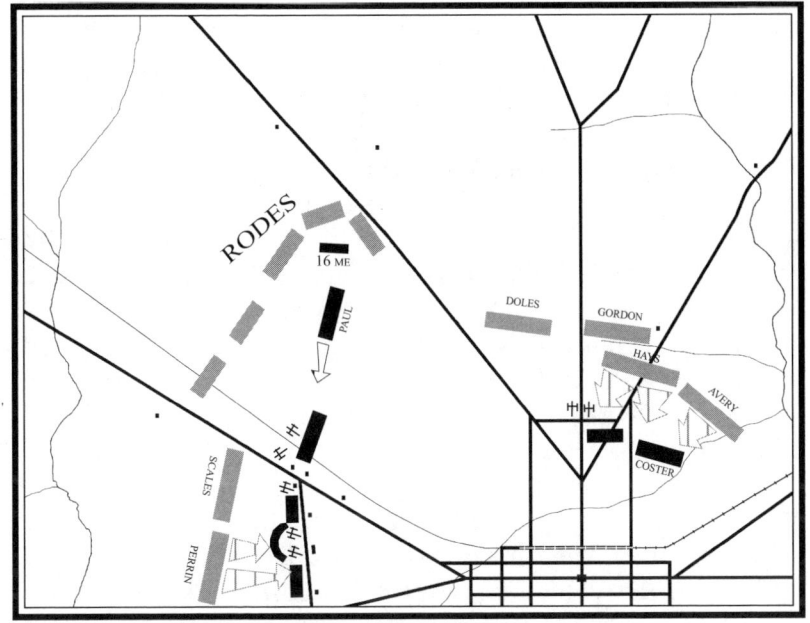

1. *Pender's Division attacks the final Union position at the Seminary.*
2. *Robinson's Division retreats from Oak Ridge leaving the 16th Maine as rear guard.*
3. *Hays and Avery overwhelm Coster at the northern edge of Gettysburg.*
4. *Doubleday has no alternative but to withdraw to Cemetery Hill.*

was approximately 2:30 p.m. when Colonel John M. Brockenbrough's and Brigadier General James J. Pettigrew's fresh brigades crossed Willoughby Run. Brockenbrough's small brigade of Virginians formed a battleline that ran south from Chambersburg Pike. Opposing them was one of Stone's regiments at the McPherson Farm and two regiments of Meredith's Brigade in Herbst Woods. Pettigrew's large brigade of more than 2500 North Carolinians formed on Brockenbrough's right facing the remainder of the Iron Brigade and Colonel Chapman Biddle's Brigade.

Brockenbrough's attack was not very aggressive in nature. Given a taste of the stubborn defense the Iron Brigade was putting up in their front, the Virginians seemed content simply to trade shots with the Federals. Assaults from Pettigrew to the south and Daniel from the north eventually caused the flanks of the Federal line to crumble. When the Yankees fell back, Brockenbrough's men kept up a steady pressure, finally sweeping them from McPherson Ridge.

While the Virginians kept the regiments in their front busy, Pettigrew's Brigade acted as the workhorse of this attack. In particular, the 26th North Carolina fought a vicious fight with the 24th Michgan and the 19th Indiana. The deadly musket fire, "...as thick as hail stones in a storm," caused very heavy casualties on both sides. But the Tarheels persistently pressed their foe. As the 26th was engaged along the front, the 11th North Carolina was able to come around the flank and roll up the Iron Brigade line. With that, the Federal position in Herbst Woods was doomed.

At this same time farther to the south, Pettigrew's other two regiments were making short work of Biddle's Brigade. With their line extending far past that of Biddle's, these North Carolinians easily flanked the 121st Pennsylvania and were able to get in their rear. After a few shots the Pennsylvanians made for the Seminary with great haste. One by one each of Biddle's other regiments was forced back to the next ridge.

With Biddle's troops leaving, the field was wide open for Pettigrew's men to attack the exposed flank of the re-treating Iron Brigade. At this critical moment, the 151st Pennsylvania Infantry was rushed forward into the face of Pettigrew's Brigade. This regiment paid a terrible price, but their action gave precious time for the brigades to their north and south to withdraw.

Exhausted and nearly out of ammunition, the brigades of Heth's Division halted their advance after clearing McPherson Ridge. Here Major General Dorsey Pender's Division took over and pushed the Confederate attack on toward the Seminary. Three of Pender's four brigades were in line from the Chambersburg Pike, running south and across the Fairfield Road. Brigadier General Alfred M. Scales' Brigade on the left and Colonel Abner Perrin's Brigade in the center carried most of the burden on this assault. General James Lane's Brigade, on the far right, south of the Fairfield Road, was distracted by Federal cavalry threatening from that area.

Scales' men had the misfortune of marching toward a portion of the Union defenses that was packed with artillery. More than 15 cannons were aimed at their front and flanks. When they had advanced approximately halfway across the fields between McPherson and Seminary Ridges the Yankee line erupted. "Almost at the same moment, as if every lanyard was pulled by the same hand, this line of artillery opened, and Seminary Ridge blazed with a solid sheet of flame...." Scales' Tarheels were immediately halted in their tracks sustaining heavy casualties. The 13th North Carolina, closest to where a section of the 4th U.S. Artillery was firing into the Confederate flank, would suffer over 70% casualties.

The left portions of Perrin's Brigade also felt the effects of the Union artillery fire and that from infantry positioned behind a breastwork that had been constructed in front of the main Seminary building. The 1st South Carolina pressed on, however, and was able to reach the Federal line south of this strong defensive position. Some of these South Carolinians now turned and fired into the rear of the breastworks. After several vollies, the Yankees started running.

The Union line disintegrated, and without reserves there was nothing Doubleday could do but order a withdrawal. The Union survivors retreated back through Gettysburg and reformed on Cemetery Hill to the south of town.

Time to start walking!

Each of the three tours is between two and three miles long, and each will take a few hours to complete. The exact time each tour takes will vary depending on the time spent viewing the numerous monuments and whether or not you follow the Excursions. Proper footwear is recommended. You should also carry a water bottle and wear a hat for protection from the sun. Please exercise caution when the tour route follows high traffic areas.

Enjoy your tour!

Tour A
McPherson's & Seminary Ridges

To begin this tour, drive to the monument commemorating the 8th Illinois Cavalry. This is the next-to-last monument on the right side before the traffic light at Reynolds Avenue and Route 30. There are parking spaces marked on the pavement at the monument. This tour is approximately 2.7 miles long.

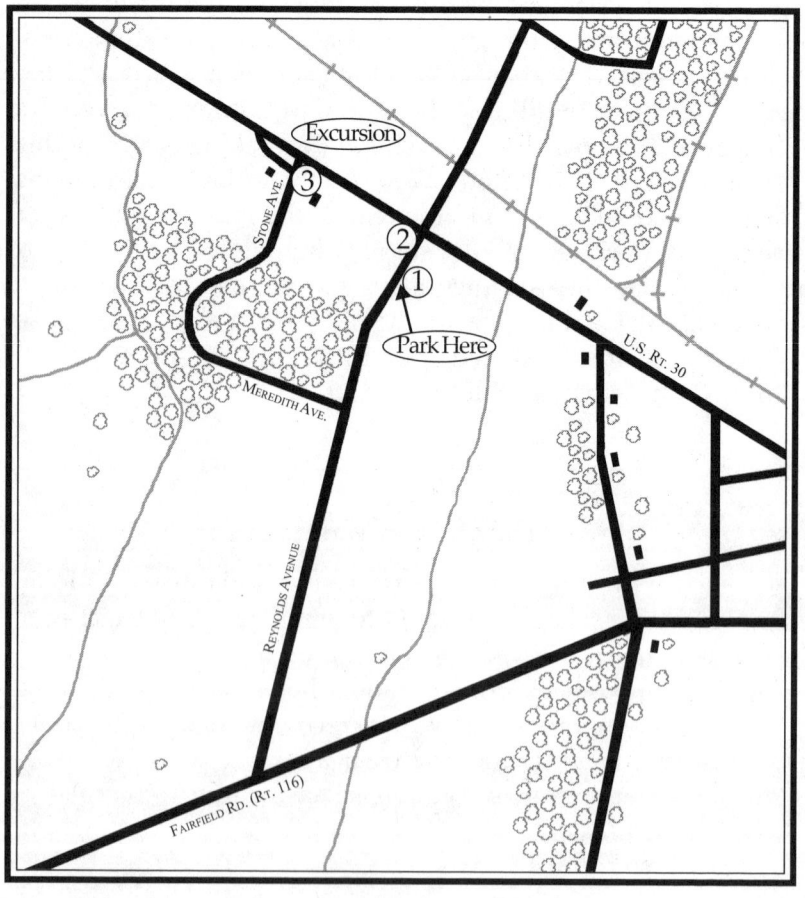

Tour A — Stops 1 through 3.

Stop A-1   8th Ill. Cavalry (Gamble's Brigade)

This is one of four monuments to Colonel William Gamble's Brigade of cavalry representing the position of their dismounted battleline. Gamble's 1st Brigade, 1st Division of the Cavalry Corps (US), contained the 8th New York and 8th Illinois, who were positioned here, south of the Chambersburg Pike, and the 12th Illinois and 3rd Indiana, who were north of the pike. This brigade was 1600 men strong and suffered 99 casualties. These outnumbered horsemen delayed the Confederate advance toward Gettysburg until relieved by infantry here around 9:30 a.m.

This monument was erected in 1891 and features a detailed depiction of a cavalry saddle on top, complete with blanket rolls and other accessories. On the back, Private David Diffenbaugh's name is listed without notation. He is singled out on the monument because he was the only member of the regiment to be killed at Gettysburg. His body rests in the Soldiers' National Cemetery.

Advanced pickets from the 8th Illinois claim to have taken the opening shot of this great battle. The "First Shot Marker" is located approximately 3 miles west on Rt. 30 and marks the spot where Lieutenant Marcellus Jones fired at Confederates approaching Marsh Creek bridge. Today this marker rests on the north side of U.S. Rt. 30 opposite the entrance to Knoxlyn Road.

From here take time to observe some of the features that figured prominently in the fighting on July 1. (To orient your sense of direction: Reynolds Avenue runs generally north-south and Route 30 runs generally east-west.) To the east is Seminary Ridge and the Seminary campus. The railroad bed and Oak Hill are to the north. Herbst Woods, McPherson Ridge and the McPherson Barn sit on the ridge to the west.

Continue on Reynolds Avenue toward the traffic light. Go to the monument on the left side of the road situated between two tall Evergreen trees.

Stop A-2   143rd Pa. Infantry (Stone's Brigade)

This and the next few stops pertain to regiments from Col. Roy Stone's 2nd "Bucktail" Brigade, 3rd Division, 1st Corps (US). This 1300-man brigade contained the 143rd, 149th and 150th Pennsylvania infantry regiments and arrived during the noon-time lull in the fighting. This was their first battle and when it was over they had suffered over 800 casualties, or nearly a 65% loss.

Initially posted beyond the McPherson Barn facing west with its brigade, the 143rd was repositioned along Chambersburg Pike facing north. Here the men confronted new threats from Rebel infantry and artillery coming from Oak Hill (where

the Peace Light now stands). From this location, the Pennsylvanians defended against advances by Daniel's Brigade from across the railroad bed. When Heth finally re-engaged from the west, Stone's units succumbed to the overwhelming numbers of the enemy on their front and flank.

This monument portrays 18 year-old Color Sargeant Benjamin Crippen. When the 143rd was finally forced to give up its hold on McPherson's Ridge and retreat toward the Seminary, young Crippen "shook his fist at the enemy and defied them to take his colors." He was shot dead.

From here walk west along Rt. 30. You should be able to walk in the grass the whole way. If the grass is too tall, walk on the shoulder of the highway—PLEASE USE CAUTION!

As you walk, you will pass the McPherson Barn and might notice the tablet mounted on its wall. It reads, "This barn was used as a hospital and sheltered the wounded of both the Union and Confederate Armies, July 1, 2, 3, 4, 1863." The barn has been restored to its wartime appearance; none of the farm's other buildings remain.

Stop A-3   149th Pa. Infantry & 2nd U.S. Artillery

Like the 143rd Pennsylvania, the 149th was initially positioned along the modern Stone Avenue facing Heth's soldiers on Herr Ridge. They too were moved to Chambersburg Pike to repulse the attacks coming from the north.

Here, while in line along the pike, the regiment received heavy artillery fire from Oak Hill and Herr Ridge. The enfilading shell fire from Herr Ridge was especially destructive. The fire was so bad that Colonel Stone ordered the regiment's flags be moved away in the hope that this would draw the enemy fire away from the regiment. The color-bearers and color-guard moved out into the center of the grassy field you see across Route 30 from where you are now standing. This small deception was successful — the Confederates redirected their fire toward the flags — and the regiment had some respite from the shelling.

From here the 149th successfully fought off portions of Daniel's Brigade; even launching its own assaults on Confederates in and around the railroad cuts.

25

Here also is the monument and cannons representing the 2nd U.S. Artillery (Calef's Battery). The battery was in line here supporting the cavalry before the morning assault by Archer and Davis. Lieutenant John Calef was replaced here by Hall's Battery when Cutler's infantry brigade arrived on the field at around 9:30 a.m. Each of these batteries contained six 3-inch ordnance rifles and spent much of their time duelling with Confederate artillery posted on the next ridge to the west. Most of Herr Ridge currently is not visible from here because of the large trees. But the field of fire was wide open in 1863.

Next is the first of many optional Excursions off of the direct tour path. If you choose to skip the Excursion, continue to Stop 4 by turning left onto Stone Avenue and walking to the 150th Pennsylvania Infantry monument.

Directly across Stone Avenue is a NPS comfort station. Here you will find rest rooms and a water fountain that are available during the summer months.

Excursion — Buford & Reynolds Memorials

Here you may want to carefully cross Rt. 30 to inspect the memorials on the north side of the highway. There you will see a bronze equestrian statue of Major General John Fulton Reynolds, a bronze statue of General John Buford, and a monument to Hall's 2nd Maine Battery. Of special interest are the four cannon barrels surrounding Buford. The barrel located to the southwest of the statue (pointing toward the comfort station) is #233 and fired the first Union artillery shot of the battle. Take a moment to read the oval plate mounted on the cannon tube.

The bronze statue of General Buford was created by James Edward Kelly (1855-1933), known as the "sculptor of American history." Other famous works by Kelly include busts of Paul Revere,

26

Teddy Roosevelt, and an acclaimed equestrian statue of Phil Sheridan. Kelly also created the reliefs adorning the 6th New York Cavalry monument you will see later.

The equestrian statue here, of General Reynolds, was created by another famous sculptor, Henry Kirke Bush-Brown. Born in Ogdensburg, NY, he died in Washington, DC, in 1935. Bush-Brown is also the creator of many famous historical sculptures located around the country. Here at Gettysburg he has four works of art: the three large equestrian statues of Reynolds, Meade and Sedgwick and a bust of Abraham Lincoln located in the Soldiers' National Cemetery.

Many significant events happened in the grassy fields here north of Rt. 30. Between here and the railroad bed the color guard of the 149th was placed to fool the Rebel artillery into redirecting their fire. On the other side of the railroad bed the 147th New York stood alone against Davis' Brigade when the two regiments to their right withdrew back to the woods on Oak Ridge. Through these same fields Daniel's North Carolinians launched multiple attacks on Stone's Pennsylvanians.

Carefully re-cross the highway and resume the tour.

Stop A-4   150th Pa. Infantry

The 150th Pennsylvania Infantry is the third regiment of Stone's brigade and spent most of the afternoon of July 1 in this area facing west in the expectation that Heth would renew his attack from Herr Ridge. At one point during Daniel's numerous assaults, this regiment wheeled to the right and cross the pike to halt the advance of the 32nd North Carolina Infantry. Eventually Heth did renew the attack from the west. Around 3 o'clock, Brockenbrough's advance, combined with Daniel's constant jabs from the north, forced the 150th to fall back to the Seminary grounds.

27

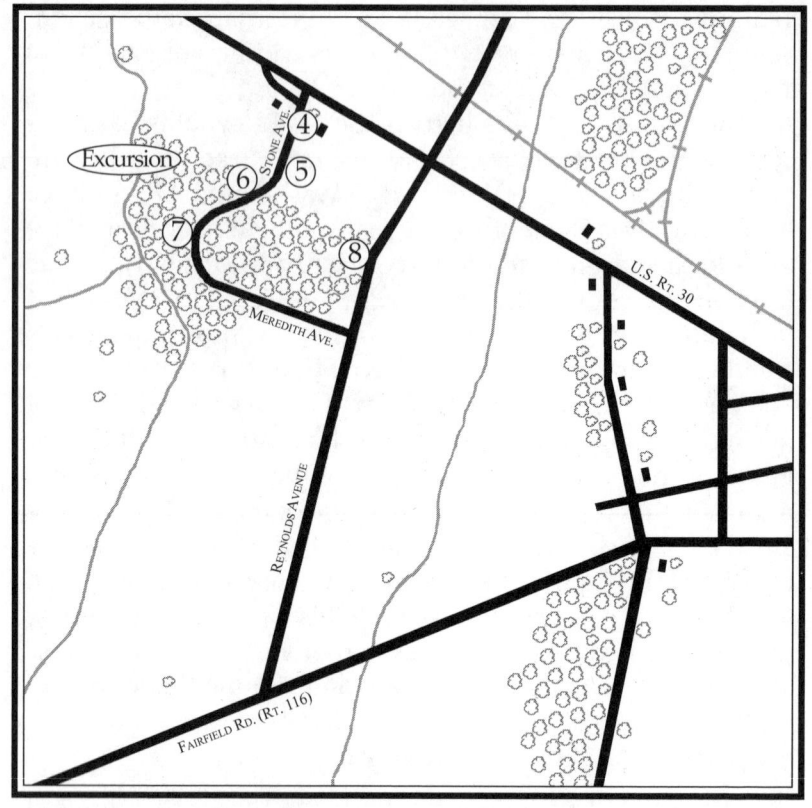

Tour A — Stops 4 through 8.

Colonel John Brockenbrough's Brigade of Heth's Division, Hill's 3rd Corps (CS), contained the 40th, 47th, 55th regiments and 22nd Battalion of Virginia Infantry. This small brigade numbered only about 970 men having been active in every fight since the Seven Days' battles around Richmond. Their losses here were just over 19%.

The small "pond" you see was here back in 1863. It is probably a small quarry hole that was abandoned once it filled with water. A couple of weeks after the battle several photographs were recorded in this area. In one shot the famous photographer Mathew Brady is seen standing at the edge of this pond.

Continue walking down Stone Avenue to the bronze statue of John Burns carrying a musket.

Stop A-5   John Burns

Most people have heard this elderly man's name in conjunction with the Battle of Gettysburg. John Burns was 69 years old at the time of the battle. He fought in this area and was wounded several times. Whatever myths have grown up about this man, it cannot be denied that he bravely fought for the Union on July 1. In November, 1863, he was personally visited by Abraham Lincoln. John Burns died in 1872 at the age of 78.

This monument features a bronze sculpture of Burns by Albert G. Bureau. A boulder from the battlefield serves as the base. A plaque quoting General Doubleday's official report describes this citizen's heroism. This memorial was dedicated July 1, 1903. It was moved from its original position when Stone Avenue was relocated further to the west.

Continue along Stone Avenue to the 7th Wisconsin monument on the right side of the road located just inside the edge of the woods.

As you walk you will pass the area where Confederate General Heth was shot in the head and rendered unconscious. Several sheets of writing paper may have saved the general's life. Folded and stuffed into the sweatband of a new hat to make it fit properly, the paper stopped the bullet. In an 1894 journal article, Heth said the location was approximately 50 yards east of the 7th Wisconsin monument.

Stop A-6   7th Wisc. Infantry (Meredith's Brigade)

Brigadier General Solomon Meredith's 1st Brigade, 1st Division of the 1st Corps (US), was made up of five regiments. The 24th Michigan Infantry joined the 2nd, 6th, 7th Wisconsin and 19th Indiana in September of 1862. These hard-fighting Westerners immediately earned the nickname "Iron Brigade" during the battle at South Mountain. Here at Gettysburg they fielded just over 1800 men, but when the fighting was over they had suffered 1153 casualties, or 63% of the brigade.

This monument is dedicated to the 7th Wisconsin Infantry and marks the right of the Iron Brigade line. The 7th Wisconsin sustained the fewest casualties in the brigade, but that was still nearly half their number. The next regiment in line, the 2nd Wisconsin Infantry, has a similarly shaped monument. One

difference is the addition of a Hardee hat. This distinctive headgear was a trademark of this tough brigade. The 2nd held the right of the line in the morning attack but, the regiments were later repositioned. They suffered a horrible 77% casualty rate. Here, in the afternoon, the 2nd and 7th Wisconsin checked the advance of Brockenbrough's Virginians until pressure from the south caused the Iron Brigade to fall back.

If you do not want to take the Excursion, follow the avenue to the bronze brigade plaque, on the right side of the road.

Excursion — The Quarry, Willoughby Run & Springs Hotel Bridge

From the 7th Wisconsin monument, you should see a faint trail through the woods paralleling the fence row. Follow this until you come to Willoughby Run. A quarry pit is to your right, on the north side of the fence. This quarry was an obstacle in the advance of Brockenbrough's Confederates, forcing them around it. This shift gave the Federals facing Brockenbrough's men (the 150th Pennsylvania) a brief respite from the southern musket fire.

Follow Willoughby Run south for about 150 yards. Look for the remains of the stone bridge abutments. Access to the Springs Hotel was by a "horse-drawn railway," and these bridge abutments and the old road bed are all that remains of the old vacation resort.

The Katalysine Springs Hotel was built in 1869. It was a four-story structure complete with a cupola to view the battlefield. This resort could accommodate 300 occupants and featured the "medicinal" springs, landscaped grounds, a lake, a billiard room, a bowling alley, and bathing rooms. It was not

Adams County Historical Society

31

here during the battle, but it does have a connection to our modern interpretation of the battlefield. It was at this hotel that John Bachelder (one of the earliest historians of the battle) first entertained a number of Civil War veterans. During these early "reunions," Bachelder traveled around the battlefield with the old soldiers marking regimental positions with wood stakes. These simple markers were the first step in memorializing the battlefield and positioning the many monuments that stand today. The resort venture failed, and the building eventually burned to the ground in 1917.

Head uphill to return to Meredith Avenue and continue to Stop 7.

Stop A-7   Archer's Brigade Plaque

Brigadier General James Archer's Brigade of Heth's Division, Hill's 3rd Corps (CS), contained the 5th battalion, 13th Alabama, 1st, 7th, and 14th Tennessee Infantry. The brigade was formed in the summer of 1861 and fought its first battle in western Virginia led by none other than Robert E. Lee. At Gettysburg the brigade numbered about 1200 officers and men. Their casualty rate was approximately 57%, most of which was from men captured (nearly 400).

This plaque details the actions of Archer's Brigade during the morning of July 1. The plaque does not mention, however, that Archer was the first general from Lee's Army to be captured. Men of the 2nd Wisconsin captured General Archer on the far side of Willoughby Run.

While here take time to look at the three monuments dedicated to the units involved in what may have been the fiercest fighting on July 1. The simple marker to the 26th North Carolina was only the third Confederate regimental marker to be placed on the Gettysburg battlefield. The 26th reported 687 casualties (over 150 killed and more than 400 wounded). This is the most casualties suffered by any Confederate regiment on any battlefield. Opposing them was the 24th Michigan and the 19th Indiana of the Iron Brigade. The 24th Michigan suffered the greatest number of men killed of all northern units engaged at Gettysburg, and the 19th Indiana lost 68% of its men. These losses testify to the hard fighting here.

Notice that the soldier portrayed atop the 24th Michigan monument wears the regulation "Hardee" hat instead of the common kepi. As previously stated, these black hats were a trademark of the brigade.

Walk to Stop 8 by following the road to Reynolds Avenue. Turn left and head toward where you started the tour. Go to the two wayside exhibits on the left side of the road.

As you walk, you get the perspective of Archer's men advancing through the woodlot in the morning. They headed this way until the Iron Brigade checked their advance, hitting them in the front and from the right. This is also the general area where the 26th North Carolina fought fiercely to push the 24th Michigan and 19th Indiana back in the afternoon. As you approach Reynolds Avenue you will pass the monument to the 151st Pennsylvania. This regiment advanced into the face of Pettigrew's Brigade, buying time for two retreating Union brigades (Meredith's and Biddle's) to reach Seminary Ridge.

Stop A-8   Reynolds Memorial

Please take time here to read the wayside exhibits. The first describes the many types of monuments and memorials

found on the battlefield. The second gives a brief account of the fighting that occurred here in the morning of July 1.

The wooded area in front of you was known as Herbst Woods at the time of the battle. (Today the names McPherson Woods and Reynolds Woods are commonly used.) The Confederate infantry had just about pushed the Union cavalry through these woods on the morning of July

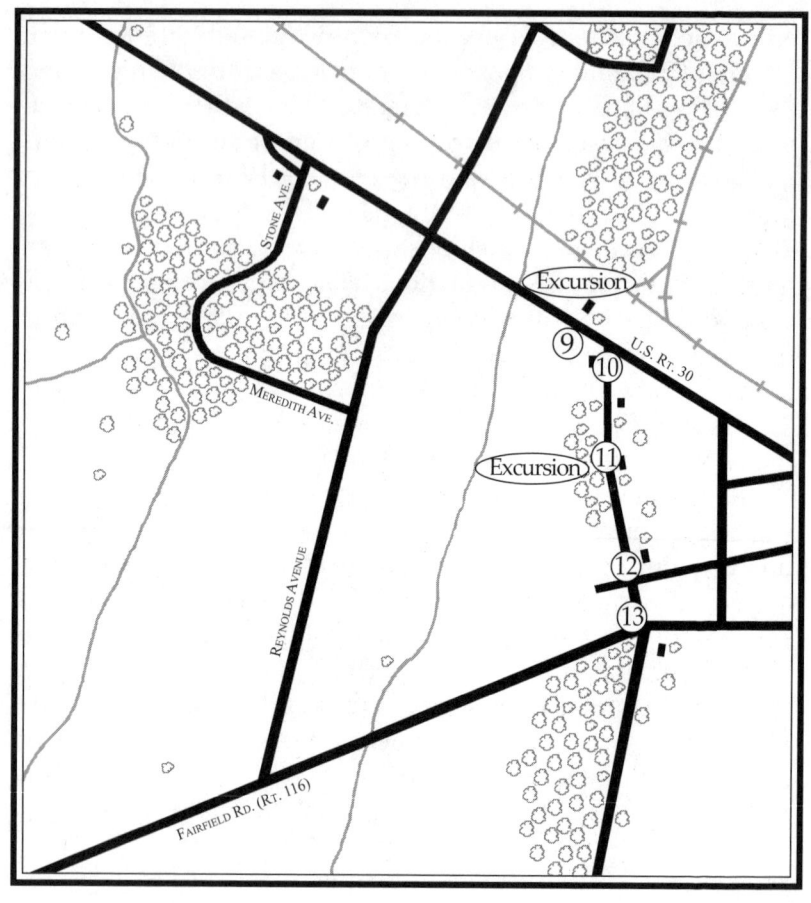

Tour A — Stops 9 through 13.

1 when the leading elements of the Union First Corps arrived. Major General John Reynolds was directing them into the fray when he was shot in the head, becoming the highest ranking officer killed at Gettysburg. You may wish to walk over and inspect the stone monument commemorating the location where General Reynolds fell.

   Proceed to Stop 9 by walking to the traffic light, turn right and walk along Route 30 until you reach a tarnished (green) cannon barrel pointing into the air.

Please use caution while walking along Rt. 30!

As you walk, imagine what it was like for the soldiers who followed this route. First, the retreating Yankees had to cross this ravine while Rebel fire hit them from several directions. Then came the Northerners' turn to fill this area with bullets and canister as the Confederates advanced across these same fields determined to dislodge the Union men from Seminary Ridge. You can see that there is no place to hide in these fields. General Scales described what his brigade faced as they descended McPherson Ridge into the low ground:

> *Here the brigade encountered a most terrific fire of grape and shell on our flank, and grape and musketry in our front. Every discharge made sad havoc in our lines.... Our line was broken up, and now only a squad here and there marked the place where regiments had rested. Every field officer of the brigade save one had been disabled....*

The 38th and 13th North Carolina regiments, who were on the left, closest to the path you are now traveling, suffered losses of over 60% and over 75% casualties, respectively.

Stop A-9   Lee's Headquarters

This vertical cannon barrel denotes General Lee's headquarters. There has been some controversy about the location of Lee's headquarters. The National Park Service favors the opinion that General Lee established his headquarters in tents pitched in an orchard that once stood on this side of the pike. However, early documentation clearly supports that Lee used the stone house across the street as his headquarters.

Here you may again choose to take an Excursion or proceed to the next stop. Get to Stop 10 by continuing along Rt. 30 to the top of the rise, turn right onto Seminary Ridge road, and stop at the driveway in front of the white house on the corner.

Excursion — Lee's Headquarters Museum &
Stewart's Battery

Carefully cross Route 30 to visit Lee's Headquarters Museum. This museum has been active since 1921. Although much of the collection has been sold off in recent years, it is still an interesting house featuring many historic pieces and relics from the battlefield. During the battle, the widow Mary Thompson lived in the little stone house which was owned by Thaddeus Stevens.

While on this side of the highway, you may also want to see the location of a section of Stewart's Battery. Walk west to the far side of the hotel property. You will see two bronze (green barrels) Napoleon cannons. From this position you can imagine the ranks of Rebels marching down the slope from McPherson's Ridge and the delight on the faces of these Yankee gunners as they blew great holes in those lines. The following is an outstanding account of what it was like to be standing here during the fighting:

Up and down the line men reeling and falling; splinters flying from wheels and axles where bullets hit; in rear, horses tearing and plunging, mad with wounds or terror; drivers yelling, shells bursting, shot shrieking overhead, howling about our ears or throwing up great clouds of dust where they struck; the musketry crashing on three sides of us; bullets hissing, humming and whistling everywhere; cannon roaring; all crash on crash and peal on peal, smoke, dust, splinters, blood, wreck and carnage indescribable....

Carefully re-cross Route 30 and proceed to Stop 10.

Stewart's Battery monument located west of Lee's Headquarters Museum. The famous railroad cut can be seen in the distance.

Stop A-10   Confederate Prisoners

Look across the street from the white house toward the stone wall. This is where the famous Brady photograph of Confederate prisoners was taken on July 15, long after the Confederate army had retreated from the area. Still commonly used in books and video documentaries to illustrate "the look" of typical Confederates from just about any time during the Civil War, it was William Frassanito who determined where this photograph was taken. In his 1975 book, *Gettysburg: A*

Journey in Time, Frassanito points out a lone tree visible in the distant horizon of the old photo. That lone tree was on East Cemetery Hill, and allowed him to pinpoint this location. The prisoners pose by the defensive works erected by the Army of Northern Virginia on July 4 when, following Pickett's failed charge, they expected General Meade to counter-attack at any moment. The stone wall here now has replaced those breastworks.

This white-washed house was here during the battle and was owned by James H. Thompson, the son of the widow Mary Thompson. In November 1862, James enlisted in the army for nine months and missed this great battle. While the fighting raged here on his front doorstep, he and his regiment, the 165th Pa. Infantry, were in Suffolk, Virginia. His enlistment ended three weeks after the battle. This historic building is currently an extension of the motel across the street, and its rooms can be rented.

The two-story, red brick house farther down Seminary Ridge on the left side is the Krauth House. It was one of the three original Seminary buildings. Charles Krauth, who became the second professor at the Seminary in 1850, lived there with his family. The house was gutted by a fire in 2004.

Continue along Seminary Ridge road to the large, red brick building with the green-roofed cupola.

Stop A-11   Old Dorm

This grand building is Schmucker Hall, but more commonly known as the "Old Dorm." It is the first of the three original buildings of the Seminary and was built in 1832. It contained classrooms, a library, a chapel, and dorm rooms. Its most distinctive feature is the copper-roofed cupola that has oxidized to the familiar green color. Famous as an observation platform for both sides, the cupola was featured in several scenes of the movie *Gettysburg*. As with most structures in and around Gettysburg, this building was used as a hospital. The building was "perforated by several balls, and large portions knocked out of the North East gable corner." Abandoned and nearly razed in the 1950s, it currently houses the Adams County Historical Society.

Here you may again take another short Excursion. If you choose to skip the Excursion, go to Stop 12 by continuing your walk along the street until you reach the Schmucker House located at the intersection of this street and Springs Avenue.

Excursion — Breastworks

Face west and walk to the tennis courts below the parking area opposite the Old Dorm. It was in this area that a breastwork was constructed by the men of Paul's Brigade before their move to Oak Hill. The breastwork was semicircular and was constructed of fence rails. This is where the remnants of the Union 1st Corps determined to make one last stand. Late in the afternoon of July 1, Pender's Division advanced across the fields directly in front of you. They received devastating fire from the Federal infantry and no less than 21 pieces of northern artillery; one Confederate claimed "they began throwing grapeshot at us by the bushel...." A regiment from Perrin's Brigade pierced the Federal battle line just to the left of this area. The Union line disintegrated as the Confederates exploited this breach in the line.

Brigadier General Alfred Scales commanded the 13th, 16th, 22nd, 34th and 38th North Carolina Infantry. Scales' Brigade fielded 1351 men and lost 704. Most of these losses were sustained in these fields (off to the right) where the North Carolinians were stopped in their tracks by the northern artillery. The four regiments of Colonel Abner Perrin's Brigade that participated in this attack were the 1st South Carolina (Provisional), 12th, 13th and 14th South Carolina Infantry. They numbered just over 1500 men, losing 593 at Gettysburg. While Scales was halted just to the north, Perrin's Brigade managed to press on. The 14th South Carolina assaulted the Union works here while the 1st South Carolina broke the Yankee line just south of here.

Stop A-12   Schmucker House

Samuel Schmucker was a founder of the Seminary and its first professor. Schmucker also founded Pennsylvania College, what is today Gettys-
burg College. This house was built in 1833 and served as his residence at the time of the battle. An artillery shell is still embedded in the wall on the south end of the house and is but a small re-

40

minder of the "thirteen cannon balls or shells [that] pierced the walls and made holes several of which were from two to three feet in length and nearly as broad."

Walk to Stop 13 at the traffic light on Fairfield Road.

Stop A-13   Shultz House

The cannons here mark the location of the Powhatan Artillery, which did not play a part in the first day's fighting. Reaching this position on the morning of July 2, they actively shelled Federal positions until late on July 3.

From here notice the Shultz house standing across the intersection, which was here during the battle but not in its current elaborate form. The stone monument on the corner in front of the Shultz house is to Company D of the 149th Pa. Infantry. These soldiers were detailed as Headquarters Guard until Doubleday ordered them into the thick of the fight to slow the Confederates. A notable casualty from this small group was Alexander Stewart; "wounded in the lungs and spine and there was not the slightest hope" for him. A young Gettysburg woman named Salome Myers would come to nurse Stewart until he died on July 6. Salome's diaries are a great primary account of civilian life in Gettysburg.

It is a long walk on this busy road to get to the next stop, so please use caution. Turn right and walk west along Fairfield Road (Rt. 116) until you reach Reynolds Avenue. Turn right onto Reynolds Avenue and stop at the three large Confederate brigade plaques on the left side of the road.

As you walk along Fairfield Road, recall that this was mostly open fields in 1863. To the left side of the road Lane's Brigade of North Carolinians were held at bay by Union cavalry as Scales and Perrin assaulted the Seminary. The Fairfield Road was the main retreat route for the Army of Northern Virginia on July 4-5.

Stop A-14   C.S. Cavalry Brigade Plaques

These three brigade plaques sitting up on the embankment are for Jones', Robertson's, and Imboden's Brigades of Confederate Cavalry, none of which were here on the battlefield of Gettysburg! Yet these plaques are some of the most visited markers on the field since they are the first that visitors see on the auto tour.

Jones' Brigade fought and defeated the 6th U.S. Cavalry at Fairfield (about 9 miles down the road) on July 3. By beating the Yankees at Fairfield, Jones secured General Lee's most direct retreat route to the west. Robertson's Brigade had occupied Orrtanna on July 3. They were not engaged with any Union forces. Imboden's Brigade occupied Cashtown on July 3. They escorted a 17-mile-long wagon train of wounded soldiers during the retreat.

Stop A-15   121st Pa. Infantry (Biddle's Brigade)

Colonel Chapman Biddle's 1st Brigade, 3rd Division, 1st Corps (US), contained the 121st, 142nd, 151st Pennsylvania and 80th New York Infantry. Here they were supported by Battery B, 1st Pennsylvania Light Artillery and Battery L, 1st New York Light Artillery — a total of ten cannons. The three regiments here (the 151st Pennsylvania was detached at the Semi-

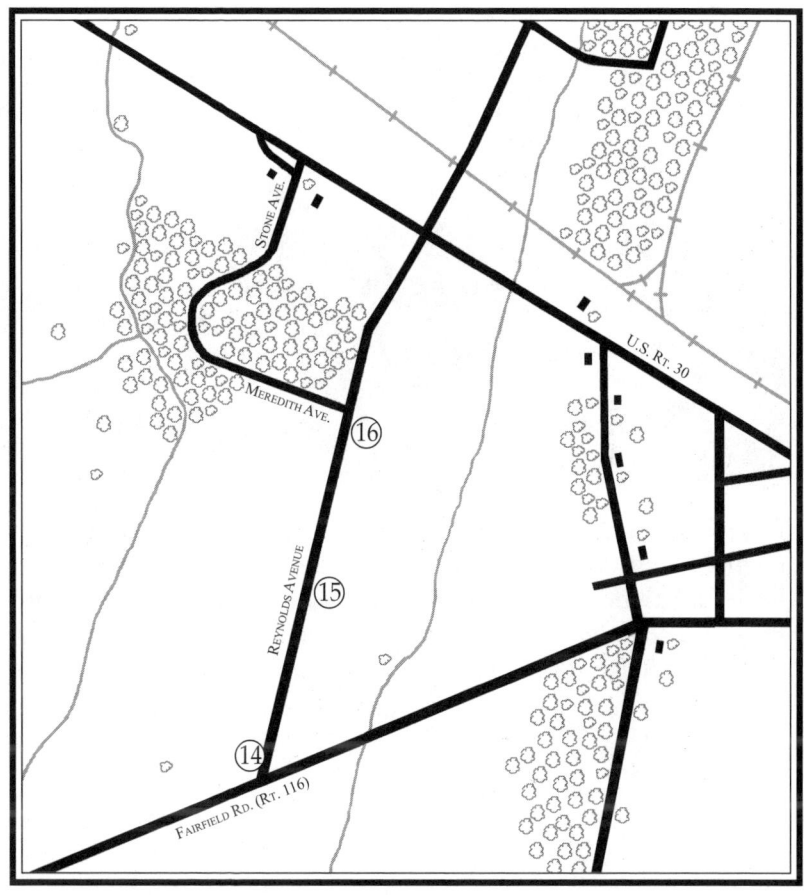

Tour A — Stops 14 through 16.

nary) fielded approximately 900 men. Their losses exceeded 60%. With the exception of the 80th New York, this was the first time these regiments had been engaged in battle.

The 121st Pennsylvania was the left regiment in Biddle's Brigade of the Union 1st Corps. The brigade was placed here to extend the Union line from the Iron Brigade's position in Herbst Woods. Here the 121st faced the 47th and 52nd North Carolina but did not fare well. The Confederate battle line far exceeded that of the Pennsylvanians. Several volleys were exchanged while the Rebels slowly enveloped their left flank. The 121st broke and ran to the Seminary buildings.

In 1887, Pennsylvania allocated funds for regimantal monuments. Many units, such as the 121st Pennsylvania, already had a monument. In this case the veterans had a new monument constructed and moved the original one to a secondary location. Several Seminary buildings are visible in the background.

Facing Biddle were portions of Brigadier General James Pettigrew's Brigade of Heth's Division, Hill's 3rd Corps (CS). This was the largest brigade in the Army of Northern Virginia with 2581 men. Of the four regiments (11th, 26th, 47th and 52nd North Carolina Infantry), only the 26th had ever experienced battle. The brigade fought hard, evident by its casualty rate of over 50%. The 26th, however, as discussed earlier, far surpassed that figure, losing over 81% of its men and giving that unit the undesireable distinction of having the greatest total loss (687), most killed (172), and most wounded (443) of all regiments in Lee's army.

The final stop of Tour A is ahead at the bronze statue of General Abner Doubleday.

As you walk, you will pass the other Union regimental monuments of Biddle's Brigade as well as the two batteries of artillery. When you reach the cannons (Calef's Battery, 2nd U.S. Artillery), notice the rough mold seams along the cannon barrels. Unlike the original barrels from this same battery around the base of the Buford statue and most others on the battlefield, these tubes are some of the reproductions that were made for the park.

Stop A-16   Gen. Abner Doubleday

Major General Abner Doubleday was born in Ballston, NY, June 26, 1819. He graduated at West Point in 1842 and served in the Mexican War and in the Seminole War. He was one of the garrison at Fort Moultrie in 1860, withdrawing with his men, by order of Maj. Anderson, to Fort Sumter, Dec. 26, 1860. He aimed the first gun fired in defense of that fort, April 12, 1861. At Antietam, his division opened the battle and captured six Rebel battle flags. When Reynolds was made commander of a wing of the Army of the Potomac, Doubleday succeeded to command of the 1st Corps. He commanded the field when Reynolds fell until the arrival of Gen. Howard. Doubleday retired from the army in 1873. He died in Mendham, NJ, January 27, 1893. Even with such a distinguished military career, Doubleday is probably better known due to the disputed legend that he invented the game of baseball.

This bronze statue was the work of Scottish sculptor J. Massey Rhind. The general's niece, Alice Seymour Doubleday, was here on September 25, 1917, to unveil the monument. Besides that of General Doubleday, Rhind created three additional bronze statues commemorating Union generals who fought here at Gettysburg: Francis Barlow, John Robinson, and Alexander Webb.

From here it's a short walk back to your car.

Tour B

Oak Hill & Oak Ridge

Park at the pull-off located on the right side of North Reynolds Avenue between the traffic light and the bridge over the railroad cut. This tour is approximately 2.1 miles long.

Stop B-1   Bridge over R.R. Cut

From here take in the view to the east and west. You are standing over the Middle Railroad Cut. There was quite a bit of fighting in this area.

This is the famous "railroad cut," where, on the morning of July 1, hundreds of Confederates from Davis' Brigade were captured after the charge of the 6th Wisconsin and the "left wing" of Cutler's Brigade (the 14th Brooklyn and 95th New York). Monuments to these three regiments are located on the southern side of the railroad here and are worthy of a moment of your time.

Look to the west. Take note of the terrain and how the railroad bed cuts through the ridges. The area before you is also where three of Daniel's regiments battled with Stone's Pennsylvanians in the afternoon. To the left, between the railroad tracks and Chambersburg Pike is the area where Union artillery was placed in the morning and the 149th Pennsylvania relocated their color company in the afternoon.

Turn around and look to the east. Notice Stewart's cannons positioned near the motel and to the right of the Oak Ridge Railroad Cut. Besides that section of artillery, there was another located in front of the woods on the left side of the railroad bed (for a total of six guns). Imagine the task before the Confederate soldiers of Daniel's and Scales' Brigades who were ordered to charge these positions in the late afternoon of July 1. The railroad cut through Oak Ridge in the distance is where the 16th Maine, almost surrounded, made its final stand as rear guard. Before being captured, the men from Maine tore the regimental flags from their staffs and ripped them to

46

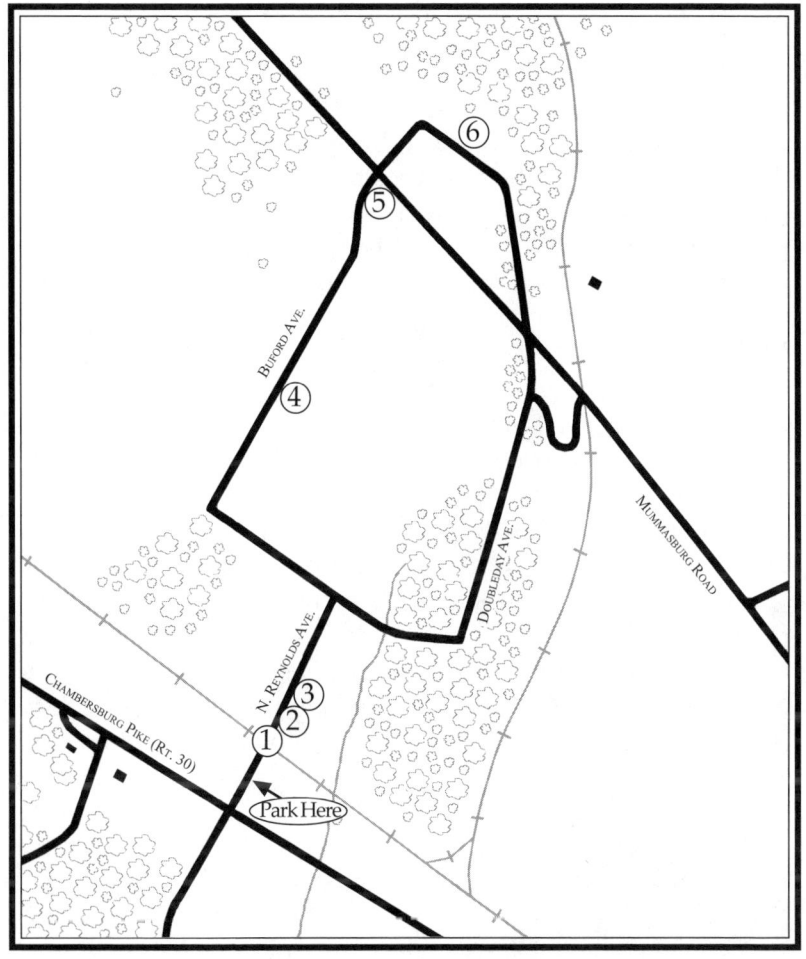

Tour B — Stops 1 through 6.

shreds rather than have them become Confederate trophies. Over 70% of the regiment was captured.

In 1996, near where you're standing, a partial skeleton of a fallen soldier was recovered. His field grave was located on the southern lip of the cut near the small flank markers for the 95th New York and 6th Wisconsin. The remains were rein-terred at the Soldier's National Cemetery.

Continue to the next stop.

Stop B-2   General Wadsworth Statue

Brigadier General James S. Wadsworth was born in Geneseo, NY, October 30, 1807. He attended Harvard and Yale college. He founded a public library at Geneseo and aided in the establishment of the school district library system. He was a representative from New York to the Peace Convention held in Washington in 1861. When it became evident that war was inevitable, he was prompt to offer his services to the government. Wadsworth began his military career as an aide to Gen. McDowell at the first battle of Bull Run. With McDowell's recommendation, he was appointed brigadier general of volunteers in August 1861 and in March 1862 became military governor of the District of Columbia. In November 1862, General Wadsworth was the Republican candidate for governor of New York, but was defeated by Mr. Horatio Seymour. In December, he was given command of the 1st Division, 1st Corps, Army of the Potomac. Here at Gettysburg his two infantry brigades (Cutler and Meredith) were the first to arrive on the field and relieve Buford's troopers. For General Grant's

Virginia campaign of 1864, Wadsworth was given command of the 4th Division, 5th Corps. James Wadsworth was killed in the battle of the Wilderness on May 6, 1864.

This bronze statue was created by Roland Hinton Perry (1870-1941). Perry sculpted one other bronze memorial here at Gettysburg, that of George S. Greene located on Culp's Hill. R. Hinton Perry has many other credits to his talent. He sculpted the bas-reliefs that adorn the Library of Congress and the Miss Commonwealth statue that tops the Pennsylvania state capitol building.

Take a moment to read the wayside exhibit here; it also discusses the fighting in this vicinity.

Stop B-3   147th NY Infantry (Cutler's Brigade)

Brigadier General Lysander Cutler's 2nd Brigade of the 1st Division, 1st Corps (US) had the 56th Pennsylvania, 76th, 84th, 95th and 147th New York Infantry engaged on July 1. A sixth regiment, the 7th Indiana, was detached on special duty that day.

Remember that Cutler divided his brigade, deploying them to support the left and right of Hall's artillery. The first monument of this "right wing" is that of the 147th New York Infantry. This regiment suffered the highest casualty rate in the brigade. This was due in large part to the fact that they were left alone in a position well advanced from where this marker is located while the regiments to their right fell back to Oak Ridge.

The next two monuments for this brigade are to the 56th Pennsylvania and 76th New York Infantry. The 56th Pennsylvania has an attractive bronze monument topped by a stand of muskets and a flag. The 56th claims the honor of firing the first infantry volley in the battle.

These regiments relieved the cavalry here in the morning and engaged Davis' Brigade until the North Carolinians were able to get around the flank of the 76th New York forcing these regiments to fall back beyond Oak Ridge.

Continue to the stop sign, turn left and follow Buford Avenue until you reach the monument to the 3rd West Virginia Cavalry.

49

Stop B-4   3rd W.Va. Cavalry (Devin's Brigade)

The monuments along this avenue represent the battle line of Colonel Thomas C. Devin's cavalry brigade. These units fled before Davis' Confederates and suffered less than 3% casualties. The 3rd West Virginia deployed here facing west with the 9th New York, 6th New York and 17th Pennsylvania to their right. This extended the cavalry line all the way to the Mummasburg Road.

This monument, positioned on the left of the brigade line, represents two companies of the 3rd West Virginia cavalry. Fielding only 59 men, it couldn't have played a large role in the fighting.

The large castle-like monument to the 6th New York Cavalry is next. This impressive monument was dedicated on July 11, 1889, and features a bronze bas-relief of the regiment in battle on the front. On the back is another bronze relief featuring Col. Devin and the regimental history. Continue to the wayside exhibit and 9th New York Cavalry monument. The

Regimental monuments of the 6th NY Cavalry (left), and the 9th NY Cavalry (above).

50

wayside discusses the role of the cavalry on this ridge. The 9th New York monument also has a large bronze bas-relief on the front. On the back is a bronze medallion of the colonel and the words, "Col William Sacket, Commanding Regiment, Killed at Trevillan [sic] Station, Va. June 11, 1864."

Take a moment to observe the area. Looking east toward Doubleday Avenue, you see the fields that Iverson's doomed brigade marched over. Baxter's men were waiting for them on the far ridge where the regimental monuments now stand. Now turn around and look to the west. In the distance are the mountains that screened Lee's army as it invaded the North. More recently, and just in front of where you are standing, stood a motor lodge called the Peace Light Inn. The Peace Light Inn was closed and razed in the 1970s.

Stop B-5   17th Pa. Cavalry

The 17th Pennsylvania Cavalry was on the right of Devin's brigade and in position here until relieved by the infantry. At that time they were re-deployed north of Gettysburg to cover the Carlisle and Harrisburg Roads. There they confronted skirmishers from Doles' Brigade until again being relieved by the infantry.

The trooper portrayed on the monument is Sergeant George W. Ferree. He was selected as the model because he best represented an "average" member of the regiment:

The left hand of art has fashioned in bold relief the horse and man, a typical soldier of the line. The face and form of the hero in granite still survives, we all rejoice in his presence today.

That day was September 11, 1889, during the dedication ceremony for this 27-ton monument.

In 1863, on the slight rise behind this monument, stood the John S. Forney farm house. The house and barn were used as a field hospital, and the Forneys reported that their farm buildings were "greatly damaged by shells." The infamous "Iverson's Pits" were also located on the 150-acre Forney farm. These "pits" were actually long burial trenches dug to hold the many bodies from Iverson's brigade. In the 1870s all of the bodies were removed and shipped to cemeteries in the south. Today, unfortunately, the "pits" are probably better known for alleged "ghost" stories than for their true significance.

Stop B-6   Oak Hill/Peace Light Memorial

The Eternal Light Peace Memorial was constructed and dedicated to peace and the reunited country. Designed by Paul Philippe Cret and featuring a bas-relief by Lee Lawrie, this memorial was unveiled during the 75th battle anniversary. On July 3, 1938, President Franklin D. Roosevelt spoke before a crowd estimated to number between 200,000 and 450,000. He then signaled for the memorial to be unveiled and the eternal flame was ignited by the sun's rays. That eternal flame lasted until 1973, when a nationwide energy crisis caused it to be extinguished. In July 1978, an electric light was fitted atop the

memorial. By 1988, the sodium vapor light was replaced, and once again an open, gas flame burns above the memorial.

After examining the memorial, take a moment and have a seat on the steps in front. Here I will describe, from right to left, the placement of the Confederate brigades in Rodes' Division, Ewell's 2nd Corps (CS). On the far right, located in the woods across Mummasburg Road was Brigadier General Junius Daniel's Brigade made up of the 32nd, 43rd, 45th, 53rd North Carolina Infantry and the 2nd North Carolina Battalion. This group lost 926 of its 2052 men at Gettysburg. The main thrust of their attacks was toward the McPherson barn visible in the distance. Next, also in the woods to your right, sat Brigadier General Alfred Iverson's Brigade containing the 5th, 12th, 20th and 23rd North Carolina Infantry. As a brigade, they suffered a casualty rate of 65%. The 23rd, however, lost nearly 90% of its members. Iverson's men refused to serve under him after this battle, and by October 1863 he had been transferred to Georgia. Positioned to the left was Colonel Edward O'Neal's Brigade of the 3rd, 5th, 6th, 12th and 26th Alabama Infantry regiments. Beginning the battle with 1688 men, nearly 700 were lost in the fight. O'Neal's poor performance at Gettysburg cost him a promotion and his command. He resigned from the army before the end of 1863. Doles' Brigade was on the far left operating against the Union 11th Corps and will be discussed in Tour C. In the woods behind the Peace Light, Brigadier General Stephen Ramseur's Brigade (the 2nd, 4th, 14th and 30th North Carolina Infantry) was held in reserve. This was the smallest brigade in the division with only 1024 men. They would eventually incur a loss of 27%.

There are some interesting things to see while wandering around the memorial. Behind and to the west of the memorial sit two unusual cannons. These two Whitworth guns were English-made cannons imported through the blockade. They feature a hexagonal bore and were breechloaders (like modern artillery). Whitworth guns were very accurate and could fire great distances, but Lee's army only had two of these. Located east of the memorial are two wayside exhibits worth reading — one points out significant features visible from here, and the other describes the memorial dedication ceremony.

Whitworth cannons at the Peace Light Memorial.

Continue along the avenue. Once through the trees you get an impressive view of Gettysburg, the college, and the 11th Corps portion of the battlefield. Recross Mummasburg Road to the next stop.

Stop B-7   90th Pa. Infantry (Baxter's Brigade)

Brigadier General Henry Baxter's 2nd Brigade, 2nd Division, 1st Corps (US), contained the 12th Massachusetts, 83rd and 97th New York, 11th, 88th and 90th Pennsylvania Infantry regiments. The 2nd Brigade reported a strength of 1452 men. They would lose 649 of them before this battle was over.

The tree-shaped monument to the 90th Pennsylvania Infantry marks the right of Baxter's Brigade. As the right flank of the 1st Corps, they fought off O'Neal's initial attack and helped defeat Iverson. One Confederate described their flanking fire as "fatal all along the line." Later in the day two regiments from Paul's Brigade relieved the 90th of its duties along the Mummasburg Road.

The 90th's granite tree is adorned with numerous bronze pieces. One piece, the bird's nest, comes from a tale that such a nest was knocked from a tree limb during the fighting. As the story goes, amid the flying bullets a member of the regiment picked up the nest full of baby birds, and returned it to its place

in the tree. The story is undocumented, but it may explain a bronze bird's nest here among the musket, cannon ball and other military items.

Take a moment to climb the observation tower and enjoy the elevated view it provides of the entire area. Also stop to read the wayside exhibit next to the tower; it points out key features of the 11th Corps line visible from here.

Proceed along the stone wall to visit the other monuments of Baxter's Brigade. The stone wall here is meant to represent the one that concealed many of Baxter's men during Iverson's attack. However, only a small segment was here in 1863. A much longer section of the wall was located across the avenue, slightly down the eastern slope. The 12th Massachusetts Infantry monument is next. It features a medallion of staunch Unionist Daniel

The Forney farm house and barns that once stood along Buford Avenue. This old photograph was recorded from the Oak Ridge observation tower.

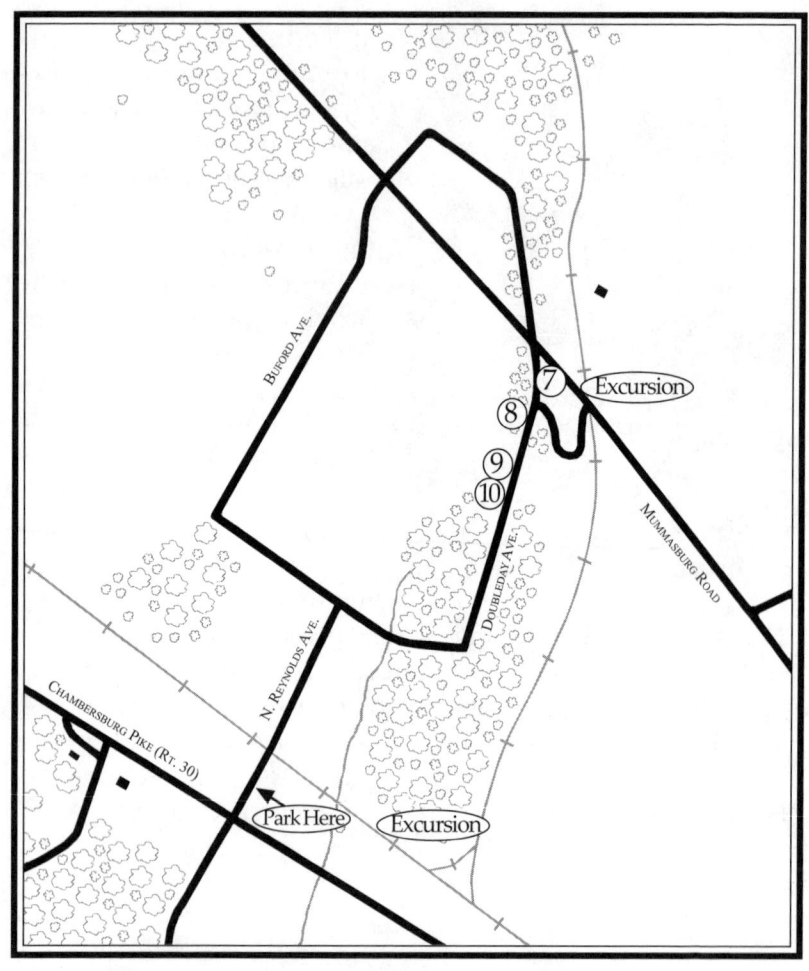

Tour B — Stops 7 through 10.

Webster and his words, "Liberty and Union, Now and Forever, One and Inseparable!" This regiment was nicknamed the "Webster Regiment" and was once commanded by Webster's son.

Excursion — Robinson Ave./McLean Farm

One of the first things of note is the bronze statue of the division commander, General Robinson. Dedicated on September, 25, 1917, this is another of the statues created by J.

Another great view from the observation tower, this one look-ing south. Visible is the field where Iverson's Brigade was smashed, Doubleday Avenue, Robinson Avenue, and the 12th Mass. Infantry monument. (Note: the height of the tower has been reduced since this vintage photo was recorded).

Massey Rhind. Rhind sculpted many war memorials and his work can also be found at Grant's Tomb and even Macy's de-partment store in New York City.

As you follow Robinson Avenue, the monuments to the 104th New York and the 13th Massachusetts of Paul's Bri-gade will be on your left. These are the two units that came up to relieve the 90th Pennsylva-nia Infantry. Both of these regi-ments faced the Mummasburg Road and were the right flank of the Union 1st Corps. Here they were under fire from O'Neal's Alabamians and were continually shelled by Confed-erate batteries. Late in the af-ternoon, they were forced to retreat when regiments of Ramseur's Brigade attacked and succeeded in getting around their right flank.

The brigade commander, General Paul, was in this area behind the 104th New York when he was critically wounded. He was shot through both eyes and permanently blinded.

The monument to the 13th Massachusetts features a likeness of Color-Sergeant Roland Morris and supposedly marks the exact spot where he fell. Sergeant Morris' company commander remembered, "across the road was a barn occupied by some of the rebels who made us their mark; and it was here and from one of their sharpshooters that Morris received his mortal wound. I saw him when he was shot; he leaped into the air and fell to the ground, struggling and crying in agony. The rebel bullet passed through his breast apparently."

Follow the avenue to Mummasburg Road and cross the tracks. A short distance down the Mummasburg Road, cross and walk up the McLean farm lane. On the right side of the driveway is a marker for the 45th New York. This stone marks the advance of the 45th when they assisted in the repulse of O'Neal's initial attack. The McLean house and barn are currently used by the National Park Service. Other than the railroad, the terrain has changed little over time.

Return to Doubleday Avenue to continue the tour.

Stop B-8   88th Pa. Infantry

The 88th Pennsylvania was positioned near the center of Baxter's line and figured heavily in the near destruction of Iverson's Brigade. One North Carolinean wrote, "when we were

in point blank range the dense line of the enemy rose from its protected lair and poured into us a withering fire." A Union witness stated, "we delivered such a deadly volley at very short range, that death's mission was delivered with unerring certainty." Baxter followed this with an order to charge those that survived. The Yankees netted several battle flags and hundreds of rebel prisoners.

Walk around the monument and out into the field. There you will find a small stone marking the location where the 88th Pennsylvania charged into portions of the 20th and 23rd North Carolina.

Here also, after the fighting, a southern soldier came upon the scene:

> There were...seventy-nine (79) North Carolinians lying dead in a straight line. I stood on their right and looked down their line. It was perfectly dressed. Three had fallen to the front, and the rest had fallen backward; yet the feet of all these dead men were in a perfectly straight line.

Next you will pass the 83rd and 97th New York monuments also of Baxter's Brigade. The 83rd New York monument is 51 feet tall. A medallion at the base reads "Ratione Aut Vi" (By Reason or Force).

Stop B-9   Sallie

The 11th Pennsylvania Infantry was the far left regiment in Baxter's line and from here participated in the repulse of Iverson's Brigade and the countercharge that followed. This unit suffered more than 45% casualties at Gettysburg, most of which were sustained during the hectic retreat from the field.

The 11th Pennsylvania has the distinction of having fought in the first and last infantry battles of the war. Following their initial three-month term of service, they were the first Pennsylvania regiment to reorganize for three years' service. This monument is topped with a six-foot-tall bronze statue of a soldier preparing to fire his musket. Because this monument is facing the field, and not the avenue, most visitors fail to see one of its most interesting features. On the front is the likeness of the regiment's mascot. Sallie, a small bull terrier, was with the regiment from early in the war until being killed during the battle of Hatcher's Run, Virginia, in February of 1865.

The 11th Pennsylvania monument featuring Sallie.

Stop B-10 — 16th Me. Infantry (Paul's Brigade)

Brigadier General Gabriel Paul's 1st Brigade, 2nd Division, 1st Corps (US), was made up of the 16th Maine, 13th Massachusetts, 94th and 104th New York, and 107th Pennsylvania Infantry. Paul's Brigade was ordered up in the afternoon to reinforce Baxter's tired men who were running low on ammunition. The brigade held this position until Ramseur's assault turned their right flank on the east slope of this ridge. The brigade entered the fight with just over 1500 men. Their casualties would total nearly 67%, losing 1026 of those men.

Here the monument to the 16th Maine is flanked by those of the 107th Pennsylvania and the 94th New York. But the 16th Maine, alone, played a critical role in the survival of the rest of Paul's Brigade. This is the larger of two monuments dedicated to the 16th Maine here on Oak Ridge. This one marks the position it was in while facing Iverson's Brigade. The other, a small marker, is back near the Mummasburg Road and shows where the regiment was ordered to make a stand, "at any cost" so that the

61

rest of the brigade could escape. While the remainder of the brigade was getting away, the 16th Maine quickly found itself in danger of being surrounded by Confederates. The regiment slowly retreated along Oak Ridge keeping up a brisk fire the whole way. Upon reaching the railroad cut through Oak Ridge, the 16th Maine was finally overrun by the Confederates. The regiment lost 232 of its 311 men.

From here you need to walk back to where you started this tour. First, you will pass the monument to the 94th New York Infantry with three bronze muskets. This regiment held the left flank of Paul's Brigade. Continue along Doubleday Avenue following it as it turns right. At the stop sign turn left onto North Reynolds Avenue and return to where you began.

Excursion — Salem Artillery

When you arrive back in the area of the railroad cut bridge, you have the opportunity to take an Excursion to a rarely visited and poorly maintained iron tablet. This unit arrived too late to play any part in the fighting on July 1, however, a section of smoothbore Napoleons spent the next two days here. The entire battery claims to have fired over 150 shells.

Warning: This Excursion takes you on unstable terrain and extreme caution should be used if you choose to visit this area. Proceed at your own risk!

From North Reynolds Avenue (near the bridge over the railroad cut) head east along the railroad tracks. Keep in mind that this is an active railway! As you reach the base of Oak Ridge (notice remnants of an old driveway that once crossed

the tracks) you need to hike up the ridge on the left (north) side of the tracks. Continue to the east side of the ridge overlooking a railroad maintenance area and Gettysburg College. Near the edge of the cliff you will see the tablet. This marker is for Hupp's Battery of the 1st Virginia Artillery. This is also the site of the controversial land-swap between the NPS and the college that resulted in the visible destruction of the Oak Ridge railroad cut. A few feet beyond this tablet, the remains of a trench can be seen among the trees. This is part of the Confederate defensive works built on July 4. General Rodes mentions these:

> During the night of the 3d, my division fell back to the ridge which had been wrested from the enemy in the first day's attack, and ... was posted so that the railroad divided it about equally. Expecting to give battle in this position, it was strengthened early on the morning of the 4th.

Carefully return to Reynolds Avenue where you parked your car.

Tour C
The Northern Plain

The third and final tour encompasses the fighting between the Union 11th Corps and Confederates from Rodes and Early's Divisions. From Mummasburg Road, turn on to Howard Avenue. Park at the second monument on the right. This is the monument to the 45th New York Infantry. This tour is approximately 2.3 miles long.

Tour C — Stops 1 through 6.

Stop C-1   45th NY Infantry (Amsberg's Brigade)

Colonel George von Amsberg's 1st Brigade, 3rd Division of the 11th Corps (US) contained the 45th and 157th New York, 82nd Illinois, and 61st Ohio Infantry. At Gettysburg they fielded 1683 men and lost over 800 casualties. Poor leadership plagued the 11th Corps throughout the battle. This brigade was posted as the left of the 11th Corps line.

This monument honors the 45th New York, an infantry regiment made up of men from New York City. The 45th was the first regiment from the 11th Corps to deploy on the battlefield. From here they advanced approximately 500 yards to the McLean farm lane where they were in time to help repell O'Neal's attack against Baxter's men on Oak Ridge.

Howard Avenue provides several good examples to discuss the placement of monuments on the battlefield. It is assumed that the regimental monuments mark the exact position held by those

units. That is definitely not always true. When many of the memorials were erected in the 1880s and 1890s, the exact areas where fighting took place were still prime farm land. And so it was here; only a small parcel of land was sold to the Battlefield Commission to construct Howard Avenue. Thus, some monuments were placed along the park road because that was the only location available. The 74th Pennsylvania and the 61st Ohio spent all their time on an advanced skirmish line. Their actual position was out in the fields toward the McLean farm, yet their monuments are the next you'll pass here on the avenue.

The crescent moon seen on these monuments is the badge of the 11th Corps.

Continue to the monument flanked by cannons.

Stop C-2   Dilger's Battery

This unit, Battery I of the 1st Ohio Light Artillery, was commanded by Captain Hubert Dilger. This battery was made up of six 12-pounder Napoleon cannons. These guns were another key ingredient to the quick defeat of O'Neal's attack on the slope above McLean's red barn seen in the distance. This battery also inflicted severe damage on Doles' Confederates during their fight with Krzyzanowski's Brigade across Carlisle Road to the right. Dilger lost 13 men wounded.

The veterans of this unit faced the same constraints as previously mentioned when it came to placing markers. Notice the flank marker across the avenue which also describes an advanced position held by four of their guns. It is evident that when the stone was being carved, the veterans did not know exactly where they would be able to place it. The appropriate distance was never filled in and the marker still reads "3   yds."

Dilger's left flank marker and Oak Hill in the distance.

While walking to the next stop (the 157th New York monument at Carlisle Road) you will pass a monument to the 82nd Illinois Infantry. This unit was not heavily engaged, being kept here to protect the two batteries of artillery. But for trivia buffs it is noteworthy that this was the only Illinois infantry regiment in the Army of the Potomac here at Gettysburg.

Stop C-3   157th New York Infantry

Posted at the Mummasburg Road on the opposite end of Amsberg's line, this regiment traversed the battlefield and alone, was fed into the fight near here. Krzyzanowski's Brigade was being roughly handled by the Confederates across the road. The 157th had the opportunity to strike an exposed portion of the Rebel line and relieve the pressure on the 2nd brigade. Unfortunately, this single regiment could do little to stop the Confederate wave that was washing away the Union 11th Corps. By the time the New Yorkers came to Krzyzanowski's aid, it was too late. Krzyzanowski's regiments were

breaking and heading for town. This left the 157th on its own and facing Confederates on three sides. Before it was over, three out of every four men in the regiment would be killed, wounded or captured. It would come as little consolation to those casualties, but this regiment was given credit for advancing farther than any other regiment in the 11th Corps.

As already discussed, the veteran's associations did not always have a choice about where to place their monuments. So it was with the 157th New York.

The text on this monument directs you to a smaller stone located 300 yards north on the Carlisle Road as the actual point of their attack on Doles.

Carefully cross Carlisle Road and continue on Howard Avenue to the next stop.

Stop C-4   119th NY Inf. (Krzyzanowski's Brigade)

Colonel Wladimir Krzyzanowski's 2nd Brigade, 3rd Division, of the 11th Corps (US), contained the 119th New York, 82nd Ohio, 75th Pennsylvania, 26th Wisconsin and 58th New York regiments. The brigade was 1420 men strong but eventually would suffer 669 casualties by the end of the battle. The brigade initially held a position behind von Amsberg's Brigade. They were ordered to this position to assist Barlow's overwhelmed division. Opposing them here was Brigadier General George Doles' Brigade, of Rodes' Division, Ewell's 2nd Corps (CS), which contained the 4th, 12th, 21st and 44th Georgia regiments totaling 1323 men. Doles suffered only a 17% casualty rate (the lowest in Rodes' Division) despite inflicting severe losses to those opposing him. The Yan-

kees exchanged several deadly vollies with the Georgians all along this line. Unfortunately the collapse of Barlow's line farther to the east, freed two of Gordon's regiments which allowed them to turn and strike Krzyzanowski's right flank. From right to left, each regiment in turn crumbled under the onslaught.

The 119th New York Infantry, positioned here, was on the left of the brigade line farthest from the flank assault. Yet their losses are typical of the brigade with 11 killed, 70 wounded, and 59 missing/captured.

Stop C-5   107th Ohio Infantry (Ames' Brigade)

Brigadier General Adelbert Ames' 2nd Brigade, 1st Division of the 11th Corps (US) was made up of the 17th Connecticut, 25th, 75th and 107th Ohio Infantry. This brigade lost over half of its 1337 men at Gettysburg. Here at Barlow's Knoll, Ames' and von Gilsa's brigades were poorly positioned and ineffectively used. General Barlow faced his divison toward Doles' Confederates to the north, leaving his right flank dangerously exposed. Barlow also deployed several of his regiments in skirmish formations, which greatly reduced their effective fire power.

Here the 107th Ohio Infantry was positioned to extend the Union line facing Doles' Georgians. The 107th was heavily engaged with Doles' and Gordon's brigades. The small cemetery behind the monument is all that is left of the Alms House that stood south east of here at the time of the battle. The Alms House was Gettysburg's "poor house." The new Agricultural Center now sits generally on the old Alms House site.

The next monument was dedicated jointly to the 25th and 75th Ohio. The 25th Ohio Infantry was especially hard hit, suffering 84% casualties (the second highest percentage of all Union regiments at Gettysburg). Here they bolstered von

107th Ohio monument in front of the Alms House cemetery.

Gilsa's thin line. As the fighting escalated, in an attempt to "check the advance of the enemy," the 75th Ohio and the 17th Connecticut were ordered to advance over the rise and down the forward slope into the enemy. Both regiments suffered heavy casualties and were quickly forced to retire with the rest of the division. The flag pole at the crest of the hill marks the spot where Lt. Colonel Fowler, commander of the 17th Connecticut, was killed by an artillery shell, "his head shot off and his brains flew on the Adjutant."

The next stop is at the crest of Barlow's Knoll where a bugler stands atop the monument.

Stop C-6   Von Gilsa's Brigade (153rd Pa. Infantry)

Colonel Leopold von Gilsa's 1st Brigade, 1st Division, of the 11th Corps (US) contained the 54th, 68th New York and 153rd Pennsylvania Infantry. On July 1, this brigade fielded less than 1,000 men. Their performance here did nothing to improve the "Flying Dutchmen" nickname they received at Chancellorsville. It is interesting to note that two of the regiments overwhelmed here by Early's attack down the Old Harrisburg Road were the same regiments on the right flank of the army at Chancellorsville two months earlier. The 153rd Pennsylvania and the 54th New York were the only two regiments facing west when Stonewall Jackson unleashed his surprise flank attack in May 1863. Their luck was no better here.

The 153rd Pennsylvania is the only unit from von Gilsa's Brigade to erect a full size regimental monument here at Barlow's Knoll.

Leading the Confederate attack on this rise was Brigadier General John Gordon's

Brigade. This 1800-man brigade was part of Early's Division, Ewell's 2nd Corps (CS), and contained the 13th, 26th, 31st, 38th, 60th and 61st Georgia Infantry regiments.

The cannons here represent Battery G, 4th U.S. Light Artillery. This battery suffered severely in an artillery duel with 12 cannons of Lt. Colonel H.P. Jones' Battery positioned a half mile up Harrisburg Road. The commanding officer, 19 year-old Lieutenant Bayard Wilkeson, was mortally wounded by one of the incoming Confederate shells. The missile killed Wilkeson's horse and nearly severed his leg. It is claimed that he finished the amputation with his own pocket knife. Before retiring altogether, the guns of this battery were withdrawn a short distance to the rear and redirected toward Doles' lines. The Union gunners fired everything they had and when they were "out of shot, shell, and case shot, used canister."

Here take another Excursion or proceed to the next stop.

To Stop 7 — Continue on Howard Avenue to the stop sign at Harrisburg Road. Turn right. Travel back toward town until you pass the shopping center and the Eisenhower Elementary School on the left. Turn left onto Broadway Street, turn right (Fourth Street) and proceed three blocks. Turn right again onto Victor Street. At the end of Victor Street turn left to Coster Avenue.

Excursion — 54th NY marker

This marker is not easy to find, and the conditions do not favor the casual walker. So be advised, in wet weather the ground is usually very wet; when tall grass is in the field, check

for ticks. If you'd still like to see 54th's marker, walk down hill angling toward the right. Look for a gap between the large pine trees. At the back of an open area amid the pines, look for a utility pole. The marker is about fifteen paces farther on in the direction of Rock Creek.

The marker shows the advanced location of a portion of

71

the skirmish line sent out by von Gilsa to face Gordon's Brigade. This small stone honors the 54th New York Infantry. Although the marker states that only "a detachment of 45 men" from the 54th was here, it was in this area that the regiment was positioned in a skirmish line. While here you may also want to continue on to view Rock Creek. Return to Howard Avenue and proceed to Stop 7.

Stop C-7   Coster Avenue

Colonel Charles Coster's 1st Brigade, 2nd Division, of the 11th Corps (US), contained the 134th and 154th New York, 27th and 73rd Pennsylvania Infantry. Coster's Brigade was released from its reserve position on Cemetery Hill to aid Barlow's Division. But, as happened repeatedly to the 11th Corps on July 1, this help was too little, too late. While enroute here, the 73rd Pennsylvania was detached and posted at the train depot. This left only three Union regiments to stop two Confederate brigades. Brigadier General Harry Hays' Brigade contained the 5th, 6th, 7th, 8th and 9th Louisiana Infantry. Colonel Isaac Avery's Brigade was made up of the 6th, 21st and 57th North Carolina Infantry. This amounted to more than 2500 Confederates facing 927 Union soldiers. The end result was probably never in doubt since the Rebels over lapped both flanks of the Yankee battle line. Much of the loss sustained by the Union regiments here was in men captured when they were nearly encircled.

Tour C — Stops 7 and 8.

Coster Avenue is only a remnant of the space once filled by the 1st brigade. In 1863, this area was mostly open fields with only a few structures. Now the town has surrounded this small parcel of the National Park. Three regimental markers are here as well as the brigade plaque. The most noticable feature is a mural that was painted on the back of an adjacent warehouse.

The mural was painted by Mark Dunkelman and Johan Bjurman. Dedicated on July 1, 1988, the painting depicts the fighting here and honors all three brigades.

Follow Coster Avenue to the right (west) to Stratton Street. From here you can take another Excursion. If you choose not to do this, continue straight on Stevens Street for two blocks, crossing Carlisle and Washington Streets. Follow the driveway into the Gettysburg College campus to the white four-story building with a cupola on top.

Excursion — Amos Humiston

To visit the memorial to Amos Humiston and his children turn left and proceed approximately two blocks south on Stratton Street. Cross the railroad tracks the stone memorial is located on the left side of the street between the tracks and the fire hall.

A few days after the battle, a dead Union soldier was found in a yard at the northeast corner of York and Stratton Streets. The body was found sitting upright, a bullet hole in his chest, and clutching a photograph of three young children. The identity of the soldier, however, was unknown. This tragic scene stirred the local community into action. The "children of the battlefield" image was widely printed in northern publications with the accompanying story. After several months, the soldier's family was located and his identity revealed. He was Amos Humiston of the 154th New York Infantry.

The publicity from the incident produced nationwide interest in creating an orphans home. In 1866, the Soldiers' Orphans Homestead was opened in Gettysburg.

Amos Humiston's body now rests in the Soldiers' National Cemetery.

While retracing your steps back up Stratton Street, stop at #218 and #221 Stratton Street to see artillery shells embedded in these two houses, directly across the street from each other. The shell at #218 can be seen in the north wall, while the shell at #221 struck the southern wall.

Continue to Stevens Street. Turn left and go two blocks, crossing Carlisle and Washington Streets. Follow the driveway into the Gettysburg College campus to the white four-story building with a cupola on top.

Stop C-8   Pennsylvania Hall

Pennsylvania College was established in 1832. In 1863, the campus consisted of three buildings: Pennsylvania Hall, Linnaean Hall and the President's house. Linnaean Hall was built in 1847 and torn down in 1942. The President's house was built in 1860 and is still standing.

The building in front of you, called the "College Edifice," the "Main Building," and more recently "Pennsylvania Hall," was constructed in 1837. The building features a 24-foot high cupola. During the battle this cupola was used by both sides as a signal station and observation post.

Each year commencement exercises are held on the steps at the north entrance to this building. Currently, Gettysburg

College has about 2,600 students from 40 states and 35 countries. The college offers undergraduate degrees in the liberal arts and sciences.

The three college buildings, like almost every building in Gettysburg, were used as hospitals. Some Union and a large number of Confederate wounded were treated here. A college student noted:

> *All rooms, halls, and hallways, were occupied with the poor deluded sons of the South. The moans, prayers and shrieks of the wounded and dying were heard everywhere.*

When finished viewing Pennsylvania Hall, follow the walking paths northwest through the campus. Walk in the direction of the fountains on the far side of the "common." At the fountains turn right, and follow the driveway out to West Lincoln Avenue. Cross and follow College Avenue north. Upon reaching the tennis courts, College Avenue curves left and becomes Mummasburg Road. It is now just a short distance to Howard Avenue where you will turn right to get back to where you started.

* * *

Hopefully you had an enjoyable battlefield tour and perhaps gained a new appreciation for the severity of the fighting on the first day of the Battle of Gettysburg.

Suggested Reading

Busey, John W., and David G. Martin *Regimental Strengths and Losses at Gettysburg*. Hightstown, NJ: Longstreet House, 1994.

Coco, Gregory A. *On The Bloodstained Field*. Gettysburg: Thomas Publications, 1987.

____ *On The Bloodstained Field II*. Gettysburg: Thomas Publications, 1989.

____ *A Strange and Blighted Land, Gettysburg: the Aftermath of a Battle*. Gettysburg: Thomas Publications, 1995.

____ *A Vasy Sea of Misery: A History and Guide to the Union and Confederate Field Hospitals at Gettysburg*. Gettysburg: Thomas Publications, 1988.

Conklin, Eileen F. *Exile to Sweet Dixie. The Story of Euphemia Goldsborough Confederate Nurse and Smuggler*. Gettysburg: Thomas Publications, 1998.

Dreese, Michael A. *The Hospital on Seminary Ridge at the Battle of Gettysburg*. Jefferson: McFarland & Co., 2002.

____ *Never Desert the Old Flag*. Gettysburg: Thomas Publications, 2002.

____ *This Flag Never Goes Down*. Gettysburg: Thomas Publications, 2004.

Dunkelman, Mark H. *The Coster Avenue Mural in Gettysburg*. Providence, 1989.

Fox, Lt. Col. William F. *New York at Gettysburg*. Albany: J.B. Lyon Company, 1902.

Frassanito, William A. *Early Photography at Gettysburg*. Gettysburg: Thomas Publications, 1995.

____ *Gettysburg: A Journey In Time*. Gettysburg: Thomas Publications, 1975.

Gallager, Gary W. *The First Day at Gettysburg*. Kent State Univ. Press, 1992.

Gottfried, Bradley M. *Brigades of Gettysburg*. Cambridge: DeCapo Press, 2002.

Hawthorne, Frederick W. *Gettysburg: Stories of Men and Monuments*. Association of Licensed Battlefield Guides, 1988.

Martin, David G. *Confederate Monuments at Gettysburg.* Hightstown: Longstreet House, 1986.

___ *Gettysburg July 1.* Cambridge: DeCapo Press, 2003.

McLean, James L. *Cutler's Brigade at Gettysburg.* Baltimore: Butternut and Blue, 1994.

New York at Gettysburg. 3 vols. Albany: J.B. Lyon & Co, 1902.

Ohio Memorials at Gettysburg. Baltimore: Butternut and Blue, reprint, 1998.

Pennsylvania at Gettysburg. 2 vols. Harrisburg: Wm. Stanley Ray, 1904.

Pfanz, Harry W. *Gettysburg — The First Day.* Chapel Hill: Univ. of North Carolina Press, 2001.

Raus, Edmund J. *A Generation on the March — The Union Army at Gettysburg.* Gettysburg: Thomas Publications, 1996.

Rogers, Sarah Sites. *The Ties of the Past: The Gettysburg Diaries of Salome Myers Stewart, 1834-1922.* Gettysburg: Thomas Publications, 1996.

Shue, Richard S. *Morning at Willoughby Run.* Gettysburg: Thomas Publications, 1998.

Smith, Timothy. *The Story of Lee's Headquarters.* Gettysburg: Thomas Publications, 1995.

___ *John Burns, Hero of Gettysburg.* Gettysburg: Thomas Publications, 2000.

Stouffer, Cindy and Shirley Cubbison. *A Colonel, a Flag, and a Dog.* Gettysburg: Thomas Publications, 1998.

War of the Rebellion: A Compilation of the Official Records of the Union and Confederate Armies. Vol. 27, Parts 1, 2, 3. Washington: GPO, 1889.

Soldier

We came together on that day, some in blue and some in grey
To battle o'er the land that lay beneath our weary feet.

The hazy glare of day's first light erased the dreams we shared last night
Of going home and fires bright spent with friends now gone.

We shared the road, a laugh, some stew. Then we charged the Boys in Blue.
When you fell I cried, it's true. A piece of me died there with you.

Many years have passed since then. Often times amongst the men
The question's asked, "Remember when?"
I always think of you my friend.

— Dave Slemmer

THOMAS PUBLICATIONS publishes books about the American Colonial era, the Revolutionary War, the Civil War, and other important topics. For a complete list of titles, please visit our website at:

www.thomaspublications.com

Or write to:

THOMAS PUBLICATIONS
P.O. Box 3031
Gettysburg, Pa. 17325

Other Gettysburg tour books from Thomas Publications:

Culp's Hill at Gettysburg

Devil's Den: A History and Guide

East Cemetery Hill at Gettysburg

Gettysburg For Walkers Only

Little Round Top: A Detailed Tour Guide

The Gettysburg Battlefield Tour Book

The Wheatfield at Gettysburg: A Walking Tour